# IT'S

# ON

# THE

# WAY

# IT'S
# ON
# THE
# WAY

## Don't Give Up on Your
## Dreams and Prayers

LISA OSTEEN COMES

Nashville • New York

FaithWords
Hachette Book Group
1290 Avenue of the Americas, New York, NY 10104
faithwords.com
twitter.com/Faithwords

Originally published in hardcover and ebook by FaithWords in August 2021
First Trade Paperback Edition: August 2022

FaithWords is a division of Hachette Book Group, Inc. The FaithWords name and logo are trademarks of Hachette Book Group, Inc.

The publisher is not responsible for websites (or their content) that are not owned by the publisher.

The Hachette Speakers Bureau provides a wide range of authors for speaking events. To find out more, go to www.hachettespeakersbureau.com or call (866) 376-6591.

Unless otherwise noted, all Scripture quotations are taken from the Holy Bible, New International Version®, NIV®. Copyright © 1973, 1978, 1984, 2011 by Biblica, Inc.™ Used by permission of Zondervan. All rights reserved worldwide. www.zondervan.com. The "NIV" and "New International Version" are trademarks registered in the United States Patent and Trademark Office by Biblica, Inc.™

Scripture quotations marked AMP are from the Amplified Bible. Copyright © 2015 by The Lockman Foundation, La Habra, CA 90631. All rights reserved. Used by permission.

Scripture quotations marked NKJV are taken from the New King James Version®. Copyright © 1982 by Thomas Nelson. Used by permission. All rights reserved.

Scripture quotations marked NLT are from the Holy Bible, New Living Translation, copyright © 1996, 2004, 2007. Used by permission of Tyndale House Publishers, Inc., Wheaton, IL 60189. All rights reserved.

Scripture quotations marked THE MESSAGE are from The Message: The Bible in Contemporary English, copyright © 1993, 1994, 1995, 1996, 2000, 2001, 2002. Used by permission of NavPress Publishing Group.

Scripture quotations marked TPT are from The Passion Translation®. Copyright © 2017, 2018 by Passion & Fire Ministries, Inc. Used by permission. All rights reserved. ThePassionTranslation. com.

Library of Congress Cataloging-in-Publication Data
Names: Comes, Lisa Osteen, author.
Title: It's on the way : don't give up on your dreams and prayers / Lisa Osteen Comes.
Description: First edition. | Nashville : Faith Words, 2021. Identifiers: LCCN 2021010629 |
    ISBN 9781546015963 (hardcover) | ISBN 9781546015970 (ebook)
Subjects: LCSH: Self-actualization (Psychology)—Religious
    aspects—Christianity. | Success—Religious aspects—Christianity. | Dreaming—Religious
    aspects—Christianity. | Prayer—Christianity.
Classification: LCC BV4598.2 .C66 2021 | DDC 248/.4—dc23
LC record available at https://lccn.loc.gov/2021010629

ISBN: 9781546015963 (hardcover), 9781546015970 (ebook), 9781546015956 (trade paperback)

Printed in the United States of America

LSC-C

Printing 1, 2022

*This book is dedicated to my remarkable mother,
Dodie Osteen, who has modeled a legacy of faith and
persistence throughout her life. Your love and compassion
for people are unmatched. I love you, honor you, and
thank you for your godly example not only to me but to
people all over the world.*

# Contents

# It's On the Way

# Foreword

We all face challenging times when we need words of faith spoken into our lives. Words have creative power. If you let them take root, they'll ignite the faith in your spirit. Because life has a way of pushing us down, if you're not careful, you will look up and realize that you're not believing as you once did. You're not passionate, not dreaming. Perhaps you have big obstacles in your path right now that you don't see how you'll ever overcome.

As one of the most inspiring and encouraging persons I know, I can think of no one better to write this book on not giving up on what God put in your heart than my sister Lisa Osteen Comes. While both of us were blessed to grow up in a wonderful faith-filled family, I have watched Lisa face seasons of trials that have tested her faith and her joy. But she allowed those struggles to shape her into an amazing woman full of faith, joy, and integrity. She is living proof to me that God can do great things in and through the heart of one who believes that his promises and answers are always on the way.

Lisa's words of faith, encouragement, and practical wisdom will inspire you as her words have so often inspired me. As always,

Lisa is transparent as she shares many of her experiences when life threw her huge disappointments and loss. Once you begin reading you will find it difficult to put down. I encourage you to read this book and embrace the words of faith and encouragement you find on every page. If you allow them to take hold and commit yourself to not lose heart and not give up, you will discover that God is moving behind the scenes and saying, "It's on the way." What God promised you is going to come to pass.

Joel Osteen

# Introduction

# Don't Give Up

Is there a dream you've been holding on to? Do you want to write a book, travel the world, start your own business, get married, have a child, or own a home? Is there a need in your life for which you've been praying? Is it related to your health, finances, or marriage? Have you been holding on and praying for these things so long that you've begun to wonder if fulfillment, healing, or restoration will ever come? My message to you is whatever you are praying about or believing God for—don't give up on those things.

I know from personal experience how easy it is to fall into discouragement or hopelessness in the time between God's promise and its fulfillment, but that is not God's will for your life. I know it gets hard, but don't you dare give up. Don't give in to fear, doubt, or worry! Hold on and have faith in God, because your answer is on the way!

There is one truth among many I hold on to in times like this: Heaven hears me the moment I pray. Heaven has heard your prayers too. Whatever breakthrough, answer, promise, or blessing you've been asking God for—it is on the way. God always hears your prayers.

Writing this book with you on my heart, I prayed for the right words to say and stories to share, because I have been through many hard times in my life too. There are things I've prayed and believed for, but as I waited for them to manifest, I became heavy-hearted and discouraged. If this is where you are today, I want you to know that the waiting season is temporary! God has greater things for you and your future. What you must focus on now is that what you are going through is subject to change. Your situation is not permanent. The answer is coming. The victory is just ahead.

God has grace for you and me that we have never experienced before. He has things in store for us that are far more than we could ever ask or imagine. He has ways of delivering you out of your problem that you can't even comprehend. The Bible says, "No eye has seen, no ear has heard, and no mind has imagined what God has prepared for those who love him" (1 Cor. 2:9, NLT). God has a wonderful future in store for you.

During the long battle with infertility my husband, Kevin, and I faced, I struggled with anxiety. I felt like I was at the breaking point in my life, like I was at the end of my rope. What I learned is that Jesus is your hope at the end of your rope! With him, you are never at the end. I heard someone say, "If you feel like you are at the end of your rope, tie a knot and hang on."

At that point in my life, I was doing everything I could to hang on. I took a break from work for a while so I could get well. I remember Kevin saying to me, "Lisa, you are going to get over this. There is nothing wrong with you."

My father said, "Lisa, I went through something similar in my forties, and I didn't think I would ever recover, but God healed me." Then he said, "You are going to make it! You have to believe me! This is temporary!"

I have to admit that, at the time, those words were hard to grasp with my mind, but I took hold of them with my spirit and with my faith. My mind was saying, *Your situation is hopeless! You're going crazy! You will never see your dreams come to pass!* But my spirit and faith held on to the promise that God was bringing me out—and he did! My father was right—it was only temporary!

With confidence, I can tell you today that what you are going through is temporary! The lack of employment you may be experiencing is temporary. The financial struggle you may be going through is temporary. The loneliness or fear you may be feeling is temporary. Your challenges have an expiration date, and you will see God's promise fulfilled if you do not lose heart and do not give up. I made it and, by the grace of God, you will make it too!

As you read through the pages of this book, I pray that you will be encouraged and strengthened to stand long enough to see God's salvation come as surely as each day breaks. May your faith and expectation for victory be restored, because you are wired for victory.

Though you may have had a bad day or a low month, you can get back up and believe again. The Bible says, "For though the righteous fall seven times, they rise again" (Prov. 24:16). Don't give up on your dreams. Don't give up on your prayers. Don't give up on one thing God has put in your heart. Defeat is not your portion. It's time to rise up into the hope and victory God has for you.

As we embark on this journey of faith together, I want you to remember God's grace and strength are working *in you*. You have the promises of God's Word to encourage you. You have God's supernatural peace to calm your fears and worries. You have the Holy Spirit inside of you. He is your helper, teacher, comforter, intercessor, strengthener, advocate, and standby.

I know the struggle that lies in the waiting. I have been there more times than I can count, but I want you to find peace in knowing that your situation is temporary. Your prayers were heard on the first day you prayed. God loves you so much, and he desires to bring you to a place of fulfillment and victory. You will rise again.

# 1

# Your Answer Is On the Way

∽

*For the vision is yet for an appointed time; but at the end it will speak, and it will not lie. Though it tarries, wait for it; because it will surely come, it will not tarry.*

—Habakkuk 2:2–3

It's easy to fall prey to discouragement when the answer to your prayer seems to be delayed. I understand. I have been in that place many times, and I want to encourage you with four powerful words: It's on the way! Whatever you are praying about today, whatever your dream is, or whatever promise God has placed in your heart, don't give up because your answer is on the way.

The verse above in Habakkuk 2 lets us know that the things we envision for our lives are for an appointed time, and though they tarry or seem delayed, we must wait for them, because they will surely come. Your dream has an appointed time. The promise has an appointed time. The answer to your prayer has an appointed time. And we are to wait on God's timing to see them fulfilled. The New Living Translation says, "If it seems slow in coming, wait patiently, for it will surely take place. It will not be delayed" (Hab. 2:3).

But waiting can be hard. It's in the waiting that we begin to doubt ourselves. We begin to doubt whether God gave us the dream. We wonder if we are really supposed to be praying for what we've been praying for. Then we begin to doubt God and wonder if the promise will ever come to pass. But God is saying, "If you wait, victory will surely come."

Of course, there are times when God performs instantaneous miracles, but usually it is after waiting on the promise that God suddenly breaks through. So we must learn to wait properly, wait in faith, and wait patiently. Isaiah 40:31 reminds us that there is strength for us even in waiting: "But those who wait for the Lord [who expect, look for, and hope in him] will gain new strength and renew their power" (AMP).

## Victory Is in Your DNA

There is another scripture that has breathed hope into my life every time I was tempted to give up. It's Proverbs 2:7–8, which says, "God holds victory in store for the upright. He is a shield to those whose walk is blameless, for He guards the course of the just and protects the way of His faithful ones."

Whenever I think about this scripture, I imagine God in heaven holding his hands as if he has something in them, saying, "Son, daughter, I'm holding victory for you. I'm guarding your life. I'm protecting you. Even though you may not see me, I am. Even though you may not feel me, I am holding victory in store for you. It is my plan for you, and it belongs to you even now. Don't be discouraged. Don't worry."

God has actually wired you for victory. He has not wired you for defeat or hopelessness.

Consider God's promises to you personally:

> But thanks be unto God who always leads us in triumph in Christ. (1 Corinthians 2:14, AMP)

> For everyone born of God overcomes the world. This is the victory that has overcome the world, even our faith. (I John 5:4)

> For the LORD your God is the one who goes with you to fight for you against your enemies to give you victory. (Deuteronomy 20:4)

> So we are convinced that every detail of our lives is continually woven together to fit into God's perfect plan of bringing good into our lives, for we are his lovers who have been called to fulfill his designed purpose. (Romans 8:28, TPT)

God always leads us to triumph when we put our faith and trust in him. He is the one who brings victory out of the ashes of your life. He has stored up goodness for you. There is no doubt that we will face adversity, opposition, and persecution, but you can always expect victory in your life because it's your spiritual inheritance, your God-given DNA.

> *You can always expect victory in your life because it's your spiritual inheritance, your God-given DNA.*

My challenge to you is this: Always plan on victory in your

life no matter what you are going through today. Take defeat off of your mind and out of your thoughts. Too many times we plan on defeat when God has promised us victory. When you plan on victory, you will receive it. Proverbs 23:7 teaches us, "As a [man] thinks in his heart, so is he" (NKJV). In other words, whatever you believe in your heart and mind, you will become. Therefore, set your faith for victory, and plan on winning the battle you are in. Plan on your dreams coming to pass, plan on God fulfilling his promises in your life, and plan on God's faithfulness because he can be trusted!

I believe that, as you embrace this challenge, the tide of the battle is going to turn for you, starting today. Your answer is on the way! Don't give up. Instead, rise up with a spirit of faith, an attitude of expectation, and a determination to trust the faithfulness of God.

## Your Prayers Are Heard

When you do finally receive an answer or a breakthrough—and you will—I want you to know that is not when God started working on your behalf. He began working the day you prayed. He is working on your child who is away from God. He is sending laborers into their pathway. He is dealing with their heart. He is working on that legal situation. He is delivering the desires of your heart.

The very moment you prayed, God heard you and heaven began to work on your behalf. One of my favorite people in the Bible is Daniel in the Old Testament. He was a godly man who had a spirit of excellence. Once he was thrown into a den of lions because he prayed to God when the king had forbidden it. God actually closed the mouths of the lions and Daniel escaped unharmed. Talk about a divine reversal! The king made a decree that everyone in his kingdom must honor Daniel's God! Daniel became a well-respected prophet and wrote one of the books of the Bible.

One day Daniel was reading the words of the prophet Jeremiah when hope came into his heart as he discovered a promise that God had given for his people. He began to pray that God would fulfill his promise to the Jewish nation. Daniel 10:12 says that the *first* day Daniel prayed, God heard his prayer and dispatched the answer with the angel Gabriel. But Daniel didn't receive the answer immediately. In fact, three weeks later an angel appeared to him in a vision and said, "Daniel, you are greatly beloved...don't be afraid. Since the first day you set your mind to humble yourself and seek God, your words were heard and I have come in response to your prayers" (vv. 11–12). It is very interesting what the angel told Daniel next. Gabriel explained that for twenty-one days he faced opposition in the spirit realm. So much so that he had to get help from the angel, Michael, and together they fought off the enemies of darkness (v. 13).

You must realize that there are spiritual forces of darkness that will try to oppose, hinder, and pressure you to give up on the promises of God. In this time between the promise and its fulfillment, you must trust that God is working behind the scenes on your behalf, refuse to give up, and keep planning for victory.

## You Are Greatly Loved

The angel spoke words over Daniel that show us how God views each one of his children. He said, "Daniel, you are highly esteemed and greatly loved." This is how your heavenly Father sees you. You are the apple of his eye and no one can snatch you out of his hand.

God cares deeply about you and knows every detail of your life. Many times, we think that the delay of the dream or the answer to our prayers is God's denial or lack of attention, but you must hold on to this eternal truth: God highly esteems and cares for you.

What the angel said next thrills me: "Peace, be strong now. Be strong." Sometimes we are at home thinking, *God, where are you? Why aren't you answering my prayers?* When, in fact, God is working on our behalf and speaking peace over our lives. In this passage of Scripture, it's as if God pulled back the veil to the spirit world and gave us a glimpse from his perspective. We may not know exactly what is happening behind the scenes, but from Daniel's story, here's what we do know:

- God always hears your prayers (1 Pet. 3:12; 1 John 5:15).
- The day you pray God dispatches the answer (Dan. 10:12).
- God is watching over his Word to perform it (Jer. 1:12; Isa. 55:11).
- We know there is a host of angels warring on our behalf (Ps. 91:11; Heb. 1:14).

God and the host of heaven are always working on your behalf. Scripture tells us that the Lord is watching over your life and he never slumbers or sleeps (Ps. 121:4). This means that while you are sleeping, he is working.

Of course we will feel discouraged or weary at times, but I want to encourage you to not overthink the situation on those days. In fact, go to bed and get a good night's rest because God promises to sustain you. When you feel stressed and the pressure to give up becomes so strong, just get it out. Voice your concerns to the Lord. Sometimes in the midst of the hardest seasons, I've said, "God, I am frustrated and stressed! I feel like giving up, but I'm not going to.

Instead, I will continue to trust you!" And then I eat some chocolate because it makes me feel so much better! Somehow chocolate ministers to my emotions. I think God made chocolate for times of stress!

But truly it is just as Psalm 55:22 says: "Cast your cares on the Lord and he will sustain you; he will never let the righteous be shaken" (NLT). In that moment of honesty and surrender to God, he will speak peace over you. He is singing songs of deliverance over you. Then when you awake, God's mercies will be new to you that morning. His grace is sufficient for you today, tomorrow, and the next day. You will find that God is faithful, and you will be okay.

## A Host of Angels

There's another part to your persisting in prayer and waiting that I want to bring out. Here's how the angel that appeared to Daniel is described: "His body looked like a precious gem. His face flashed like lightning, and his eyes flamed like torches. His arms and feet shone like polished bronze, and his voice roared like a vast multitude of people" (Dan. 10:6). These same magnificent angelic beings are watching over you. They are ministering spirits sent to serve you (Heb. 1:14), and like the angels ministered to Jesus in the Garden of Gethsemane—at his lowest point—angels are ministering to you and working on your behalf. (See Luke 22:43.)

> *Powerful things happen in the spirit realm when you pray. You set miracles in motion. All of heaven begins to move on your behalf.*

Powerful things happen in the spirit realm when you pray. You set miracles in motion. All of heaven begins to move on your behalf. When you pray, angels are dispatched and your answer is released. Because God watches over his Word, he also commands his angels to war until his promises are fulfilled. Just as Gabriel called for backup and brought Michael in to fight off the forces of evil set against Daniel's prayer, so it is that angels assigned to you will not relent and will overpower the opposition to get you to victory.

God is fighting for you in the spirit realm. He is pushing back the darkness. He is defeating your enemies. All around you are angels, ministering spirits, whom God has assigned to you. You may not be able to see them, but you must trust God.

Angels are so real. We must be aware of the fact that we're not alone. Not only are God the Father, Jesus, and the Holy Spirit with us, but we also have a host of angels accompanying us. The Bible indicates that a third of the angels fell to the earth and followed Satan (Rev. 12:4). This means two-thirds are still in heaven and on earth working on our behalf. As the Scripture proclaims, "Those who are for us are more than those against us" (2 Kings 6:16).

Joyce Meyer once told a story about a woman who had brought her reluctant husband with her to one of Joyce's meetings. He did not want to be there and was not enjoying himself, so he sat there through worship like a bump on a log. When Joyce finally came up and began to speak, he panicked and said, "Who are all those men with Joyce?" His wife looked up at the stage and then back at her husband and said, "There are no men with Joyce." He said, "Yes, there are. They're all standing around her in a semicircle. And when she opened her Bible, they all pulled out their swords and lifted them up."

This man was seeing the angels of God encamped around Joyce. God had caused him to see into the spirit realm. Did he ever become a believer that day!

There's a similar story in 2 Kings 16, where the prophet Elisha was being pursued by a mighty army. Elisha's servant was afraid, but the Bible says, "Elisha prayed, 'O Lord, open his eyes and let him see!' The Lord opened the young man's eyes, and when he looked up, he saw that the hillside around Elisha was filled with horses and chariots of fire." Unseen to natural eyes, those fiery angelic spirits delivered victory to Elisha that day, and they are warring for your victory today. Psalm 103:20 tells us that angels excel in strength as they hasten to fulfill God's Word.

## Plan on Victory

I can't tell you how many times in my life all of these scriptures that I've shared with you have greatly encouraged me as I walked through my own challenges. I've seen the faithfulness of God in my life time and time again. I was born with a severe birth defect, and the doctors told my parents I would never walk or talk. I had absolutely no muscle tone in my body, could not move my neck or limbs, and had no sucking reflexes, which meant I could hardly eat. What I had was similar to cerebral palsy. I'm beyond grateful that my parents did not give up on me or the promises of God. Instead, they turned to the Bible, had faith that God heals today just as he did in Bible times, and prayed for me. God completely healed me before I was one year old.

You may have heard about another time later in my life when my faith was put to the ultimate test. In 1990, a package was sent to my father at Lakewood Church. It was my job to open my parents' mail at the time. When I picked up this particular package, I did not know that I was about to open a pipe bomb filled with shrapnel and ten-inch nails. When I lifted the last piece of tape on the flap of the box, it exploded. I heard a deafening boom and, through my shock, I thought I was dying. But I came to my senses and realized that not only had I survived, but that I also only had minor injuries compared to what could have happened to me. I could have died, but God protected me. His angels were surrounding me that day. I often say jokingly that Satan tried to kill me with a bomb, but now I am the bomb!

When I was in my early twenties, God proved himself faithful yet again when I went through an unwanted divorce. Everything in me told me to give up. I was depressed and hurt, and even thought my dream to be in ministry was over. I felt disqualified. It seemed like I was drowning in shame and hurt, but I pressed through the discouragement and refused to give up, and God restored my life and purpose. With time and healing, I met the love of my life, Kevin, whom I've been married to for over thirty years as of the writing of this book. (You can read these stories and more in detail in my book *You Are Made for More!*)

After God healed my heart and Kevin and I settled into our life, we began to try to have children. We weren't having success on our own, so we sought the help of fertility doctors. For several years we went through infertility treatments and I had two surgeries before our doctor told us he couldn't help us anymore. It was a very difficult time, but the first thing Kevin said to me was, "Our hope has always been in God and not man!"

So what did Kevin and I do next? We *planned* on having children anyway. We took hold of God's promises and began to pray and declare what he said about us in the Bible: "God makes the barren woman keep house and to be a happy mother of children" (Ps. 113:9). Our declaration was, "Children are a reward from God and our children will be mighty in the land" (Ps. 127:3; 112:2).

When we bought our first house, we made sure we had a couple of extra bedrooms for the children we were *going* to have. We bought a piano because we believed that one day one of our children would play the piano. One time, we received a sample package of diapers in the mail. It had two diapers in it, and Kevin brought it to me and said, "Look what came in the mail—two diapers! We are going to have twins!"

After eight years of believing and not giving up, God blessed us with twin girls and a son at the *appointed time*. We adopted our children from Mercy Multiplied, an amazing ministry led by our dear friend Nancy Alcorn that helps unwed mothers and girls who are struggling with challenges. We didn't even have to apply for adoption. God supernaturally brought them into our lives. It was such a miracle!

During those eight years, when we could not see it, God had a plan and he was working on our behalf. He was working behind the scenes, bringing us the children he ordained for us to have. And I am so glad I didn't have to go through nine months of pregnancy, then the labor and delivery! I got my children, and I got to keep my shape!

Kevin and I still have that package of diapers today. It's a reminder of the faithfulness of God. And our daughter Catherine plays the piano.

Throughout my life—through fear, heartbreak, betrayal, and infertility—God has been faithful to his Word. As I walk with the Lord, more and more, I am learning how to take hold of God's promises found in his Word. I am learning to take them as truth beyond the reality I see with my physical eyes or feel with my emotions. I am learning, day by day, the importance of praying and declaring the truth of God's Word. Speaking God's Word rather than rehearsing our hardships magnifies God over any of the challenges we face.

## You Will Never Make It Talking Like That

I remember a time, twenty-nine years ago, when Kevin and I went on a mission trip to India with my dad, my brother Joel, and his wife Victoria. Though I was excited about going, this trip proved to me that I was still learning the power of my words.

My father had made many trips to India, and his ministry work there had greatly impacted the country. I was thrilled to be a part of this endeavor. Our objective for this trip was to speak to hundreds of leaders and pastors who had gathered from all over India, but somehow along the way the vision for the trip grew a little blurry for me.

In order to get to the place where we would speak to the leaders, we had to ride in a bumpy van for three hours. It was so hot and dusty. I was just ready to get to the hotel and get cleaned up and settled.

We were planning to stay in what they called a government hotel. It sounded so official and nice, but when we arrived in this remote village, I knew things were not going to be quite what we thought. The so-called hotel was basically concrete walls and two old twin beds. The ripped mattresses were one inch thick and filthy. There were lizards and roaches crawling around, and the bathroom was so dirty that I didn't take a shower for the five days we were there because I felt like I was cleaner than the bathroom. One night we came back to our room and there were roaches all over our bed!

There was one bright side in all of this. I had spotted the cutest monkeys in the trees and that made me happy. I've always loved monkeys and even wanted one as a little girl. But as soon as I said something about the cute monkeys, the host said, "Beware of the monkeys. They are dangerous!" Needless to say, I was not a happy camper.

Now, listen, I am a city girl. Just give me a nice hotel, and I'm good. But God knew what he was doing.

I loved teaching the people during the day but dreaded going back to the room because I could not sleep at all. I kept saying to Kevin, "This is awful! I can't sleep here! I don't think I can make it for five days!"

After two days of complaining, Kevin said to me, "Lisa, you need to quit complaining and change what you are saying. You'll never make it talking like that."

Well, it made me mad, but I knew he was right. So I decided that, every time I thought about quitting, I would say, "I can do all things through Christ who strengthens me! I can do this! I am on a mission from God!"

## Check Your Words

The Book of Proverbs teaches us that death and life are in the power of your tongue and what you say matters (Prov. 18:21). Our words have power. We can talk ourselves out of something or talk ourselves *into* something. We can talk ourselves out of victory or talk ourselves *into* victory. You—not anyone else—have the power to set the tone and atmosphere of your life with your own words. You have to think about what you are saying because many times our words are draining us and working against us.

> *We can talk ourselves out of victory or talk ourselves into victory.*

During those first two days in India, I kept saying, "I can't do this. I can't make it," but Kevin reminded me that I had to take the emphasis off of me and put it on God. Often, we measure ourselves against the problem, but the battle belongs to the Lord (2 Chron. 20:15) and nothing is too difficult for him (Jer. 32:27).

I changed what I was saying, and I was able to sleep better that night. The next night, I had such peace and slept like a baby.

On the last night of our trip, I woke up slightly because I felt the bed shaking, but then I quickly went back to sleep. Soon, Kevin woke me up a little panicked and said, "Lisa, do you feel that? I think it's an earthquake!"

I surprised myself when I said to Kevin, "I think you're right," and I turned over and went back to sleep.

I will mention that Kevin stayed up worrying. I told him the next morning he needed to quit complaining and trust God! We learned there had been an earthquake many miles away and we were feeling the tremors, but I had entered into a supernatural peace that only God can give, and I was unafraid and had no desire to give up anymore.

## Don't Dwell on the Circumstances

If you feel like you want to give up all the time, you may be focusing on the circumstances. The Bible teaches us to fix our eyes on Jesus, the author and perfector of our faith (Heb. 12:2). It's necessary to receive prayer and talk things out with someone you trust, but if you find yourself rehearsing the situation over and over, you will become discouraged.

There comes a time when you must start rehearsing the Word of God, dwelling on what God says, and prophesying your own future by declaring God's Word. What I learned from my trip to India was that I had to change the way I was thinking and talking. I needed to get into agreement with God's Word and allow him to sustain me. I learned that I couldn't speak defeat and expect to get victory. My negative words were discouraging me and making things worse. I also learned that I had more in me than I realized. And so do you.

When you feel like giving up, remember you have supernatural reinforcements. God's grace and strength are available to you. God will give you supernatural peace that passes all understanding. It's a peace that only God can give.

You can be going through the worst of trials or the worst of storms, but the storm doesn't have to be inside of you. The Holy Spirit dwells on the inside of you. He is your helper, teacher, comforter, and advocate. He is your strengthener and standby, waiting to help you at any time.

## Keep Fighting

I want to encourage you to keep on fighting the good fight of faith, because that is exactly what your enemy, Satan, wants to steal from you. He wants you to lose faith in God and give up on your dreams and prayers. What we must remember is that we don't have to defeat Satan because he is already defeated. Your responsibility is to enforce Satan's defeat in your life by resisting him and his lies.

One of the greatest truths I ever learned as a young adult was from John 10:10. Jesus taught us that Satan has a plan to steal, kill, and destroy us, but God's plan is for us to have an abundant life. I always knew that God had a plan for my life, but when I learned that Satan also had a plan for my life, that was a game changer. It lit a fire in me and a determination to never give in to Satan's plan for my life. I choose God's plan. I choose abundant life and I refuse to believe the lies of the enemy over God's powerful Word and promises.

One of the ways you can stay encouraged is to not tire of doing what is good. Galatians 6:9 says that if you don't get tired and don't give up doing what is good, you will reap a harvest of blessings. What could God mean by this?

Perhaps he is saying, "Don't get tired of going to church. Don't get tired of serving others. Don't get tired of praising. Don't get tired of praying. Don't get tired of speaking the Word, even though it seems to be delayed. Those things are good, and they are making a difference. You are pushing back discouragement and the forces of darkness."

I like to say it this way: When you don't know what else to do, just keep doing what you know to do. Don't get weary of doing what is good. Those are the things that are making a difference, and at just the right time—the appointed time—you will reap a harvest.

## Grace Like Manna

Do you remember the story of how God fed the Israelites manna from heaven? (See Exodus 16.) Every morning, they would wake up to a fresh blanket of bread covering the earth. God had instructed them to go out and get only what they needed for that day and no more. They could not store it up for the next day, else it would spoil and be eaten by maggots.

Just like that manna, God's grace is given to you brand new every day. Its sustaining power is sufficient for this day only. Don't spoil it by worrying or thinking about if you will still have enough strength and grace for tomorrow or the next day. Just walk in God's grace for today. We can get anxious and worried when we start looking ahead. We need to do like the Israelites did, and pick up our grace for the day and trust that God is going to sustain us as we wait for the victory he has stored up for us.

Hebrews 10:35 reminds us: "Don't cast away your confidence in God; it will be richly rewarded. You need to persevere so that when you have done the will of God, you will receive what he has promised." If you will keep your trust in God, you will receive the answer. You will be richly rewarded. Continue to persevere knowing that God will sustain you. Your dream has an appointed time, so wait for it, because it's on the way!

## PRACTICAL APPLICATION

*Encouraging thoughts and scriptures to meditate on:*

- I am wired for victory and not defeat. Proverbs 2:7–8 says, "God holds victory in store for the upright."

- My dream has an appointed time, and I will trust God's timing. Habakkuk 2:2–3 says, "For the vision is yet for an appointed time; but at the end it will speak, and it will not lie. Though it tarries, wait for it; because it will surely come, it will not tarry."

- God is renewing my strength as I wait on him. Isaiah 40:31 says, "But those who wait for the Lord [who expect, look for, and hope in him] will gain new strength and renew their power" (AMP).

***Practical steps you can take:***

- Instead of worrying and giving up, I will depend on God's grace and mercy to sustain me each day.

- I will guard my mouth and choose to speak words of faith and hope, aligning my words with God's Word.

- I will not give up because my answer is on the way!

# 2

# Let God Fight Your Battles

❦

*Do not be afraid! Don't be discouraged by this mighty army,*
*for the battle is not yours, but God's.*
                                    —2 Chronicles 20:15, NLT

I love the stories in the Old Testament because they encourage us and build our faith. Romans 15:4 says, "These things were written in the Scriptures long ago to teach us, to give us hope and to encourage us as we wait patiently for God's promises to be fulfilled." I want to remind you that the men and women we read about in the Bible, who accomplished great feats, conquered giants, and changed nations—they too had to wait for their promise. One such person was a man named Jehoshaphat, one of the kings of Judah, and I think his story will encourage you and give you hope.

Jehoshaphat's story shows us what we can do during this time between the promise and its fulfillment. In 2 Chronicles 20, three armies had gathered to attack the people of Judah, and Jehoshaphat didn't take this news sitting down. No, he was just like you and I are when we get bad news—he was alarmed! He was afraid, but he resolved to inquire of the Lord, calling the people together for a time of prayer and fasting.

When Jehoshaphat began to pray, he said, "God, you are powerful and mighty; no one can stand against you!" He totally focused his attention on God and his greatness, rather than the vastness of the three armies lined up against him. Wow! Jehoshaphat is teaching us how to respond in faith and not fear, and that faith and prayer set miracles in motion. Then God began to speak to the people of Judah through a man named Jehaziel. He said, "Do not be afraid! Don't be discouraged by this mighty army, for the battle is not yours, but God's. You will not even need to fight. Take your positions; then stand still and watch the Lord's victory. He is with you, O people of Judah and Jerusalem."

That was all Jehoshaphat needed to hear. He appointed some men to lead their army, singing and giving praise to God. That's when God caused the enemy armies to turn on each other and kill one another. As God had spoken, Judah did not even have to fight the battle.

Let me ask you: Are you fighting a battle that belongs to God? Are you striving and stressing over the answer to your prayer or solution to your problem? Have you allowed fear to overtake you because of your circumstances? I think we have all been guilty of this. I admit I have been there, and this is why I love this story.

What a powerful miracle God performed on behalf of King Jehoshaphat and the Israelites. Jehoshaphat had a problem, but he also had a promise from God, and he and the people of Judah prayed and praised their way through it. I see these three Ps—promise, prayer, and praise—as a key to winning the battles of life. Just as God frustrated the plans of their enemy, he will do the same for you. You won't even have to be on "attack" mode or "do-it-myself" mode because as you hold on to God's promise, continuing to pray and praise God, he will bring the victory. Why don't you stop and take a deep breath right now and declare, "God, I know you are fighting my battles for me! You are bringing the victory!" When you have a problem, take God's

> *When you have a problem, take God's promises and continue to pray and praise your way through it.*

promises and continue to pray and praise your way through it.

This is what God is saying to you now in the midst of your challenges: "Don't be afraid or discouraged. I am with you, and I am going to fight this battle for you."

The story of God winning the battle for the Israelites that day is full of principles we can apply to our lives as we wait in expectation knowing the answer is on the way. I want to share six of them with you.

## 1. Use Your Spiritual Weapons

The Bible teaches us that we have an enemy who wants to destroy us. First Peter 5:8–9 says, "Stay alert! Watch out for your great enemy, the devil. He prowls around like a roaring lion, looking for someone to devour. Stand firm against him, and be strong in your faith."

Sometimes we find ourselves in a spiritual battle because our enemy, Satan, comes into our lives to steal, kill, and destroy (John 10:10). Though he is our defeated enemy, he is still on the prowl and wants to wage war with God's people. He comes to steal our faith in God and his Word and to steal the promise and the dream God has placed in our hearts. That's why the Bible teaches us to fight the good fight of faith. Don't give up on the promise God has given you. Hold on to it! Don't get involved fighting against people because we don't wrestle against flesh and blood, but against spiritual forces of darkness (1 Tim. 6:12; Eph. 6:12).

The apostle Paul instructed believers to "put on all of God's armor so that you will be able to stand firm against all the strategies of the devil...so you will be able to resist the enemy in the time of evil. Then after the battle you will still be standing firm" (Eph. 6:13). Remember, Satan is already defeated. So in order to maintain your position of victory, you must use your God-given weapons. You can resist the lies of Satan and meditate on God's Word. You can resist the enemy, in the name of Jesus, and refuse his plans for your life. You can continue to praise and worship God in the battle, because this confuses the enemy! As you pray, Satan's plans are frustrated.

As I mentioned before, I went through many years of treatment for infertility. At one point, I began to experience anxiety and have depressive thoughts and panic attacks. It was like it all came out of the blue. It was such a dark time in my life. I knew the hopeless feelings were an attack from the enemy and that he didn't want me to come out of that season with my faith intact. As you may imagine, there were times I felt like giving up. I felt like staying home, but I knew I had to fight the good fight of faith. Those were the times when I would pull out my spiritual weapons. I spent more time in the Word of God, the sword of the Spirit, than I ever had before because I knew I needed to encourage myself. I needed to remind myself of the promises of God.

His Word helped me cut through the lies the enemy was throwing at me. It gave me the strength to resist those lies and helped to align my thoughts with God's thoughts. When he would tell me I would never have children, I

> *The Word is YOUR SWORD to cut through the lies of Satan.*

fought back with "He settles the childless woman in her home as a happy mother of children" (Ps. 113:9).

The next thing I began to do more than ever was pray. I prayed and asked God for direction, and he sent me a great doctor to get the help I needed. Then I made a decision to spend more time praising and worshipping God—even though nothing had changed—*yet.*

Like Jehoshaphat and the people of Judah, as I praised and worshiped God, things began to change. It didn't happen overnight, but eventually that heaviness over my life broke. Anxiety lost its hold, and I came out in victory. God was so good. I would not have been able to come out of that season if I did not use my spiritual weapons. God frustrated the plans of the enemy and blessed us with three children!

You too must use the spiritual weapons God has given you because this is a spiritual battle we are in. Don't allow your defeated enemy to bully you or talk you out of your blessings. Your victory is on the way!

> *Don't allow your defeated enemy to bully you or talk you out of your blessings.*

## 2. You Are Surrounded by God

You may be facing some difficult challenges, but none of those things move God one bit. Absolutely nothing is too difficult for him. You may be surrounded by negative circumstances, negative people, negative everything, but if God be for you who can be against you?

I have always relied on the Book of Psalms for encouragement. When I was facing anxiety, I would meditate on verses like Psalm 125:2, which says, "As the mountain surrounds Jerusalem, so God surrounds His people from this time forth and forever" (NKJV). You may feel overpowered or overwhelmed by the enemy, but God has your enemy surrounded! He promised to bless you and surround you with favor. (See Psalm 5:12.) The enemy may be surrounding you, but he has to go through God first, and he is surrounding you with favor, provision, and protection on every side. You are surrounded by God.

One of my favorite verses is Psalm 32:7, which says, "You are my hiding place; you shall preserve me from trouble; you shall surround me with songs of deliverance" (NKJV). God, and the heavenly hosts, are singing songs of deliverance over you right now. Can you hear them?

When I think of this, I imagine God saying, "No, Satan, you are not going to have my child. No, Satan, you are not going to touch them. They belong to me and you have no legal right in their lives!" Isn't that beautiful? You may be surrounded, all right, but you are surrounded with songs of deliverance. Chime in and start singing with God.

God also promised to surround you with his great mercy. Psalm 32:10 says, "But he who trusts in the Lord, mercy shall surround them" (NKJV). You see, the enemy is outnumbered. You are surrounded with protection, mercy, favor, and deliverance. What you're going through does not move God, so don't let it move you. Be steadfast, immoveable, as Scripture says, always abounding in the work of the Lord (1 Cor. 15:58, NKJV).

## 3. Keep Your Focus on God

The third thing we learn from Jehoshaphat is that you must keep your focus on God. This is so important, and he shows us how to do this so well. Through this Bible retelling, we are able to witness how he focused his attention not on the enemy armies but on his God. We see this right away with the first words that came out of his mouth. He said, "Lord, the God of our ancestors...power and might are in your hand, and no one can withstand you" (2 Chron. 20:6).

He weighed the situation: on one side, he saw the armies gathering against him. On the other side he saw God. He made the choice to go with God.

It really is a no-brainer when you think about it, because what you are going through right now is nothing in comparison to who God is. This is where the power of perspective comes into play. It changes everything.

In order to be decisive like Jehoshaphat was and in order to be confident in God's power over your enemies, you need to get the right perspective. You need to know that God is bigger than any weapons that try to form against you. He is all-powerful, and nothing is too hard for him.

In 1981, my mother was diagnosed with liver cancer. She had gotten so sick and looked frail and jaundiced. The doctors told us that she only had a few weeks to live. But my mother kept her focus on God and his words. I remember she would go around the house all the time, saying, "I will live and not die and declare the works of the Lord." If we drove by a graveyard, she would say, "I will live and not die." She would quote John 10:10: "The thief comes to steal, kill, and destroy, but God came that I might have abundant life."

There was a point in all of this when she simply put her Bible on the floor, stood on it and said, "God, the only thing between me and death is your Word, and I believe your Word—that by the stripes of Jesus I am healed." Those few weeks the doctors gave her have grown into forty years. At the writing of this book, my mother is full of energy at the age of eighty-seven!

My mother believed God was bigger than that death sentence. Won't you believe today that God is bigger than anything you are facing?

Whatever you magnify becomes bigger in your own sight. Whatever you magnify is the overpowering influence and force in your life. If you are overpowered by worry, fear, and the circumstances that surround you, then maybe you are magnifying those things instead of magnifying God.

> *Whatever you magnify—becomes bigger in your own sight.*

So often we pull out the mirror instead of the magnifying glass and we start looking at ourselves and how weak we are. We speak to ourselves saying, "Oh, no, you are way too weak. You're not going to make it. How are *you* going to do it? It's all on *you*. We look at ourselves.

Not only do we magnify our weaknesses at times, we magnify our problems or the enemy. "Oh, man, it looks like Satan has the upper hand," or "Wow! Look at those circumstances. There is no way I can overcome this."

But you know what we need to do instead? We need to put the mirror down and change the direction of the magnifying glass. We need to focus it on God, so we can then say, "Wow, God, you are magnificent. You are all powerful. Nothing is too difficult for you."

> *When you focus on how big YOUR GOD IS, then it's a NO-BRAINER!*

You need to magnify the Lord and make him bigger in your eyes.

## 4. Don't Allow Fear to Overcome You

The next lesson we learn from Jehoshaphat's example is not to allow fear to overcome us. Fear always causes us to imagine the worst. My good friend Irene travels with me when I preach. We were on a trip one time, when she told me that her shoulder had been hurting and it was bothering her because she is a hair stylist and uses her arms all day.

On this trip, Irene went for a walk and her shoulder began to hurt again. She noticed that it was affecting her hip too. One side of her body seemed to be pulling down. Then she noticed she was walking with a limp.

Fear took hold of her and she began to think, *Something is wrong with the whole side of my body now!* She got really concerned and convinced herself that she was sick and needed to go back to her room and go to bed.

When she got back to the hotel room, she took off her shoes and realized that she was wearing two different shoes—one flat and one with a slightly higher heel! A pain in her shoulder turned into a major health problem—in Irene's mind! That's how fear works!

First John 4:18 says that fear brings torment into your mind and life, but God's Word says, "A mind controlled by the Spirit is life and peace" (Rom. 8:6). When we keep our mind on God's thoughts, we will be full of hope and life and peace.

It truly is so easy to give in to fear and worry when we're hit by bad news, but I want to encourage you with this: instead of allowing yourself to be overcome by fear, train yourself to say, "No. God, I will trust you. I will not be afraid."

No one is immune to fear, but it's what you do in that moment that determines your outcome. Instead of giving way to fear, determine to set yourself to inquire of the Lord and to seek his plan and strategy.

When I was in my twenties, I experienced the worst turbulence on a flight that I had ever encountered. The storm was strong, the winds were tossing the plane back and forth, and I was not only alarmed, I was nauseous. I was never so glad to be on the ground as I was when we landed because I had doubted whether we would even make it home safely. Needless to say, after that flight, I wasn't thrilled to get on a plane anymore. I have always loved to travel, but the fear that came against me was fierce.

I knew I had a choice. Would I give in to fear and refuse to fly again? Or, would I fly even though I felt fear and expect God to help me? I also knew my destiny was at stake because part of my purpose is to travel and speak. Not to mention that I love to travel the world, and by giving in to fear, I would allow fear to steal that joy from me.

So as you can guess, I chose to get on the next airplane with fear and trembling. It wasn't easy, but conquering fear is well worth it. I chose to trust that God would take care of me even though I was very nervous. It took a few trips, but on each flight, I began to relax more and more. And since that time, I have continued to travel and enjoy it immensely!

During that season, I learned that I first had to identify the source and purpose of fear. Hint: The source of fear is not God. It's Satan. Second Timothy 1:7 says, "God has not given us a spirit of fear, but of power and of love and of a sound mind." Again, if it's not from God, then it's from the enemy and you can respond by resisting it and acting against it. Let's not allow fear to torment our minds or paralyze us from moving forward. You have too great of a purpose and future ahead of you.

When you set yourself to seek the Lord instead of giving way to fear, you will hear from heaven. God will give you wisdom and direction as you seek him. The Bible says, "If any of you lacks wisdom, you should ask God, who gives generously to all without finding fault" (James 1:5). In Jeremiah 33:3 God said, "Call upon Me and I will answer you and show you great and mighty things that you do not know." So, instead of panicking, choose to trust God and you will experience his faithfulness.

## 5. Remind God of Your Covenant Promises

The Bible is full of God's covenant promises that, through Christ, belong to us. God has given us these exceeding and great promises, and as God's Word says in Isaiah 62:6, "Put the Lord in remembrance [of his promises], keep not silence" (AMPC). Jehoshaphat did this as he inquired of the Lord. He said, "God, Abraham was your friend, and you gave him this land. I want to remind you that I am the seed of Abraham. You made a covenant with him and I am a part of that covenant. You said that if calamity comes on us, then you would deliver us."

Jehoshaphat pulled on his covenant promises and his inheritance as the seed of Abraham. We are also the seed of Abraham, so those promises are ours too. Because of this, we can be bold in our prayers with God. We can say, "Lord, this is what your Word says. I'm bringing my case before you." Like Jacob held on to the angel at Bethel, we can hold on to God and not let him go until we see our promises fulfilled. (See Genesis 32:26.)

Jesus told a story in Luke 18 about what it means to pray and never give up. He talked about a widow who sought a just judgment from an unjust judge. This judge turned a deaf ear to this woman again and again, but she would not give up. Finally, she wore the judge down! He said, "*I don't fear God or care about people, but this woman is driving me crazy. I'm going to see that she gets justice, because she is wearing me out with her constant requests!*"

He would not have given the widow what was rightfully hers if she had not been persistent in reminding the judge of her plight.

Like this widow, we should continue to pray and never give up. It is also important to know that no matter how the enemy tries to misrepresent God's character, God is not like the unjust judge in this story. It is God's good pleasure to give us the desires of our hearts. He says, "Come to me, and I'll give you what you need. Come to me, and I will fulfill my promises to you."

We don't have to beg him. We only need to remind him, which really blesses us more than anything else. Reminding God of his Word, reminds us that we are not hopeless, that we are not without help, but that we have the promises of God.


## 6. Don't Be Moved by Your Inabilities

Looking deeper into Jehoshaphat's story, we learn not to be moved by our inabilities. Jehoshaphat demonstrated this lesson by being very honest. He said, "God, we do not know what to do, but our eyes are on you" (v. 12).

Many times, when we are faced with uncertainty, our minds race. We question. We doubt. We wonder how it will all work out. We try to think of things we can do to solve things on our own. But you know what? We need to stop. Let's not go there. Let's be like Jehoshaphat and say, "God, I don't know what to do, but my eyes are on you."

There is nothing like saying, "God, I trust you." When you have that posture, God will speak to you. He will show you what to do.

Because Jehoshaphat had a heart of humility, prayer, and faith and because he did the right things even as the wrong things were happening to him, God began to move on his behalf. He began to speak to the Israelites. He said, "Do not be afraid or discouraged because of this vast army" (v. 15).

God is saying this to you now: "Don't be discouraged. Don't be afraid because of what you see or because of what you are going through."

God wants you to be encouraged. The word *discouraged* means "to take courage out." Sometimes when things come against us, they knock us down. They knock the wind out of us and take the courage out of us. God is saying, "It's not what *you* can do, but what I can do." You can be strong and courageous because God will help you.

The next thing God said to Jehoshaphat was "the battle is not yours, but God's. . . . You will not have to fight this battle" (vv. 15–17). In other words, he was saying, "Let me handle this for you."

If you are a parent, you can really connect with God here. Has anyone ever mistreated your children? It really does something to you, doesn't it? You want to jump in and immediately fix the situation. I believe that's the way God is with us. I can imagine him saying, "Hey, excuse me. You're messing with my kid, and I'm going to handle this."

> *Let go and let God do his thing.*

The next thing God did for the Israelites was expose the enemy's plan. He said, "Tomorrow march down against them. They will be climbing up by the Pass of Ziz, and you will find them at the end of the gorge in the Desert of Jeruel."

God gave Jehoshaphat inside information—supernatural intel!

When you serve God, the Holy Spirit will reveal things to you that you need to know. Things that no one could have told you but God! That's what happens when you set your heart to seek the Lord!

The final thing God did as a result of Jehoshaphat's humility, prayer, and faith, was to say, "Take up your positions; stand firm and see the deliverance the Lord will give you, Judah and Jerusalem. Do not be afraid; do not be discouraged. Go out to face them tomorrow, and the Lord will be with you" (v. 17).

Jehoshaphat obeyed God and set out toward the enemy armies, but before he did, he decided to appoint certain men to go out before the army of Israel. He appointed them to sing praises to the Lord and to worship him for the splendor of his holiness.

So now, in front of the armies of the Lord, these men went out, saying, "Give thanks to the Lord, for His love endures forever" (v. 21).

All this and they hadn't even faced the army yet. They didn't know the outcome, but they trusted God. They sent these praisers and worshipers before them. What we learn here is that when the odds are against you, take your position.

> *Position yourself with worship, praise and thanksgiving*

What is your position? It's a posture of worship, praise, and thanksgiving. Sometimes we think we have to sweat it out and do all the work, but God is just saying, "No, I want you to march out. I want you to take your position and begin to praise me. Thank me and worship me."

When we don't understand, we can say, "Father, my position is one of praise. My position is one of thanksgiving. My position is one of worship, because I believe you are bigger than anything I'm going through."

So as the people of Judah took up their positions of prayer and praise, the Lord set ambushes against the enemy and they destroyed one another! Not one person escaped (v. 23)!

All they had to do was march and praise. Some of us need to quit working so hard and start marching and praising. We need to get up and quit worrying about things and just march and praise. March and praise until you see the enemy frustrated! March with strength and confidence. March with courage and praise God, because you trust him and know that he will fight the battle for you.

As you praise him, he will turn things around. As you praise God, he will give you inside information. As you praise God, he will frustrate the enemy's plan. As you praise God, he will cause the enemy that comes against you one way to flee in seven ways. That's what God did for the Israelites. Praise and worship in the midst of a spiritual attack is the highest expression of faith. It's telling God that, instead of giving in to fear, you are going to trust and praise him.

If you read the whole story, you will see that God didn't just deliver the Israelites, but he also rewarded them greatly. They were able to gather up all the spoils, equipment, clothing, and other articles of value. There was so much that they had to stop gathering because it was too much for them to handle. So Jehoshaphat named it the Valley of Berakah, which

> *God will turn your battlefield into a blessing field.*

means blessing. The takeaway here is that God took their battlefield and made it a blessing field.

As it was with the Israelites, Satan is also trying to destroy you in the valley, but God will cause you to be blessed in the valley. I pray Jehoshaphat's example helped and encouraged you to quit trying to work so hard. Shake off all that worry and anxiety. Stop giving in to fear and allow God to fight your battle for you because victory is on the way!

# PRACTICAL APPLICATION

## *Encouraging thoughts and scriptures to meditate on:*

- God is fighting my battles for me! Second Chronicles 20:15 says, "Do not be afraid! Don't be discouraged by this mighty army, for the battle is not yours, but God's" (NLT).

- I am surrounded by God's mercy, favor, and deliverance. Psalm 32:10 says, "Many sorrows shall be to the wicked; but he who trusts in the Lord, mercy shall surround them" (NKJV).

   Psalm 5:12: "Surely O Lord, you bless the righteous and surround them with favor as with a shield!"

   Psalm 32:7: "You are my hiding place; you shall preserve me from trouble; you shall surround me with songs of deliverance" (NKJV).

- God is frustrating the plans of the enemy as I maintain a posture of prayer and praise. Second Chronicles 20:22 says, "At the very moment they began to sing and give praise, the Lord caused the armies of Ammon, Moab, and Mount Seir to start fighting among themselves" (NLT).

## *Practical steps I can take:*

- I will keep my focus on God and his ability, and not my inabilities or my circumstances.

- I will not allow fear to rob me of my joy or purpose.

- I will resist fear and trust God to fight my battles for me.

# 3

# When You Don't Know What to Do

❦

*We do not know what to do, but our eyes are on you.*
—2 Chronicles 20:12

One of my favorite things about the story of Jehoshaphat that we studied in the last chapter is that Jehoshaphat didn't try to hide behind false confidence. His humility led him to follow the pattern of any other faith-filled but out-matched person: go directly to God. He admitted that with all that was coming at him, he just didn't know what to do. What plan is there when your troops are outnumbered by not one but three armies looking to make war? Despite what it looked like to the natural eye, God met Jehoshaphat with grace and a strategy that gave him victory over his enemies.

In the same way, whatever you are facing today will be met with God's grace when you turn to him in humility, knowing he has all the answers. Train yourself to do this first. If you've had trouble trusting and have been used to giving in to fear or panic, going to God first is your new default. It is now the first thing you do when you don't know what to do.

There's another man in the Bible that I want to tell you about. The odds were stacked against him in ways many of us have never seen in our modern lives. The man is David. In 1 Samuel 30, he came home to quite a surprise.

## The Root of the Problem

David was a great man of God and hero in the faith, but he had his share of trouble. He had a lot of problems and enemies. One of his enemies was King Saul. Saul was jealous of David and was trying to kill him. As we come upon this story in 1 Samuel 30, we find that David and his army had been out fighting their own battles, which is hard enough on its own. But when they got back home to Ziklag, things got drastically worse. While they were away in battle, their homes were left vulnerable and unprotected. Another enemy came in and took their wives and children captive. The Bible says that "David and his men came to the city, and, behold, it was burned with fire; and their wives, and their sons, and their daughters, were taken captives. Then David and the people that were with him lifted up their voice and wept, until they had no more power to weep" (vv. 3–4).

Could you imagine? Maybe you've been in a similar place before where you wept until you couldn't weep anymore. Maybe you are there now. But here's what I want to tell you: That is about to change! Your turnaround is coming, and things are going to shift in your favor. God is about to turn the tables on the enemy. You may not see how close you are, but I'm telling you it is time to dry your tears. There is something so powerful in David's experience that you need to grab on to today.

Verse 6 says, "And David was greatly distressed for the people spoke of stoning him, because the soul of all the people was grieved, every man for his sons and for his daughters." You can see how the situation just went from bad to worse. David's men were so grieved that they blamed him, their anointed leader, for their loss even though he was not responsible for it. He was hurting right along with them. His family had been taken as well.

The sad reality that their response exposes is that, in the darkest of times, we tend to look for someone to blame. Many times, that person is ourselves. But the blame game doesn't get us anywhere. It only adds to our problems. We have to get down to the root of the problem if we are going to get victory. The root of the problem is this: we have an enemy who wants to steal, kill, and destroy us. He wants you to stay down and discouraged.

In moments like these we have a choice: we can blame others and go down the path of self-pity. Or, we can do what David did, which we can see, starting at verse 6 again:

> ...but David encouraged himself in the LORD his God... and David inquired at the LORD, saying, Shall I pursue after this troop? Shall I overtake them? And God answered him, Pursue: for you will surely overtake them, and without fail recover all... And David recovered all that the Amalekites had carried away: and David rescued his two wives. And there was nothing lacking to them, neither small nor great, neither sons nor daughters, neither spoil, nor any thing that they had taken: David recovered all. (vv. 6–19)

What has the enemy stolen from you? God is speaking to you through David's story that he is going to help you recover all! David's story also tells us that you cannot recover all if you just sit around doing nothing and weeping until you can't weep anymore.

At some point, even when it seems like we don't know what to do, there are things we can do. Let's look at those now.

## Don't Give Up!

David could have given up when he found out he and his men had lost their families and possessions. Can you imagine coming home from one battle only to find out you lost everything? Then to have your own people turn on you—and want to kill you—when you'd lost just as much as they had? David could have really given up here, and I don't know how many of us would have blamed him. But he didn't!

Hanging in there and not giving up is a key decision you have to make in the battles of life. Making the determination that you're not going to give up, back down, or blame God marches you closer to victory faster than you may realize. Satan's plan for your life is that you give up on your dreams, desires, and whatever you are praying about. He wants to wear you down, and sometimes the pressure to give up is so strong. It's emotional pressure. It's spiritual forces of darkness pressing against you. And it is real, but it doesn't have authority over you. You have authority over that pressure and hopelessness in the name of Jesus!

Satan may have his plan, but God's plan for you is victory and restoration. His plan is for you to recover all!

Several years ago, Joel, Victoria, and I were asked to visit a high-profile person in our city who was going through a public divorce. The woman welcomed us into her home, and we listened to her, encouraged her, and then prayed with her. She explained how she had never been depressed or unable to sleep in her life, but recently she had been taking medication for both. Before we left, she said, "Do you really think God can get me through this?"

We said, "Yes, he can, and he will if you will trust him."

Honestly, it didn't look like we encouraged her much. She still seemed so distraught, but there's power in prayer! I gave her my contact information, but never heard from her.

Two months after our visit, I was surprised to see her in church and asked her how she was doing. She said, "Lisa, I was so depressed and ready to give up when you came to my house. But after you all prayed and left, something lifted from me. I don't even need my medicine or sleeping pills anymore because I have been sleeping like a baby ever since!"

She was a different person! She had felt such pressure to give up, but she pressed through it! That was in 2003, and I can tell you that I witnessed the favor of God on her life as she faced every challenge and God enabled her to recover all. Today she is happily remarried and free from the pain of the past! Just like my friend, you can press through with God's help.

Not too long ago, a friend and I were talking with another woman about how she had lost her entire savings and how she was feeling suicidal. She told us that she felt pressure to kill herself. We prayed with her and encouraged her, and took authority over the forces of darkness.

Over those next few weeks and months, I made it a point to stay in contact with her. In that time, she went from not working at all and almost losing her home to working eighteen hours a day. Though life has been challenging for her, I witnessed her transformation into a completely different person. She became so joyful and free.

During one of our visits, I asked her if she had suicidal thoughts anymore. She laughed and said, "No, I can't even believe I thought about doing that. It was like a demon spirit telling me to kill myself."

Friend, that is exactly what it was. I will say this again. The enemy will have us blaming everything and everyone else except him, when he is the one who comes into our lives to steal, kill, and destroy. The root of our problems is this: We have an enemy who wants to keep us down and discouraged, and he will see to it by any means necessary.

The hopelessness that he tries to hold over us is at the root of this suicide issue that's been so heavy on my mind lately. It is so prevalent today—even among Christians.

A recent news story told of a twenty-five-year-old mother who committed suicide. She wrote on her Facebook timeline before she did it and asked people to forgive her. Then she took her three children and drove her car into the river. One of her sons survived. He slipped out through the window. When the police went to him for a statement, he said that, as soon as they hit the water, his mother got out of her seat and said, "Oh my God! I have made a huge mistake!" She tried to get them all out but couldn't.

I tell you this story because it shows how Satan always lies to you. When the battle has gone on for a long time and you are weary, he tells you that the only way out is to kill yourself. But as this mother found out, Satan is always wrong. God is always right. Believe what God is telling you. Don't give up on God. Don't give up on yourself and the bright future God has waiting for you. He loves you so much. I hope you can hear him now, saying, "I have great plans for your life! You are going to recover all!"

## Encourage Yourself

Learning how to encourage yourself is so important because on a day-to-day basis, it's just me, myself, and I. No one can really feel what you feel or know what you are going through. People can relate to you and pray for you and encourage you. We need that. We can go to church two or more times a week—and we have to have that. But when you go home and you have to face another day with the same problem and live with the same person—who may be your problem—you can feel all alone and discouraged all over again.

You may know what I am talking about. You come home from church, where you got pumped up and full of faith, but it seems like you lose it as soon as you walk in the door, because you are reminded of all the problems you have. Nighttime is another time when things look bleaker than they really are. It's in these times when knowing how to encourage yourself is vitally important. This is when you need to be able to call on God and fight back the lies of the enemy with the truth and light of God's Word.

To begin with, here is a scripture that will help you at night-time. It's Psalm 3:5–6. It says, "I lie down and sleep; I wake again, because the LORD sustains me. I will not fear the tens of thousands drawn up against me on every side."

When you think you can't make it, God promises to sustain you again and again. Just go to bed and wake up again. Then when you wake up, you will realize that, just as Lamentations 3:22–23 says, his mercies are new every morning! You will also realize you did make it and you will continue to make it. That's God's promise to you.

Here are a few more practical ways you can encourage yourself when you are alone.

### 1. Recognize when you first start feeling discouraged.

Don't wait until it's so bad that you can hardly get out of bed. Start to recognize that downward spiral and catch it before it gets out of hand. And then, as they say, don't go there. Stop and say to yourself: "I am not going to go there. I am going to encourage myself today!"

### 2. Do something immediately to combat the discouragement.

In Psalm 43:5 the Psalmist recognized he was headed in the wrong direction and he said this: "Why am I so discouraged? Why so sad? I will put my hope in God! I will praise Him again—my Savior and my God!"

The psalmist talked to himself, and he made a U-turn in his attitude. He said, "I have a lot of questions, but I am not going down this road of discouragement. Instead, I am going to praise God again and again and again. I am going to trust him." One of the most effective things you can do is to stop and say: "Father, I am going to take time to praise you because you are all-knowing and all-powerful, and my trust is in you."

### 3. Resist the enemy.

Jesus said in Luke 10:19: "I have given you authority over all the power of the enemy and nothing shall by any means hurt you." The Amplified Bible says, "I have given you physical and mental strength and ability over all the enemy possesses." You are already equipped to overcome the attacks of the enemy.

So one of the first things you can do when you feel discouragement is say: "Satan, I recognize that this is a scheme of yours to make me give up, and I resist you in the name of Jesus. I am not going to take your bait!"

James 4:7 says, "Resist the devil and he will flee from you."


*4. Stay on the offensive.*

So many times, we are on the defensive—we're busy putting out fires! But you can be prepared and have your battle plan ready for when discouragement comes so the fires don't even start! You can have your arsenal ready, which can consist of:

- Listening to inspirational and faith-filled messages on your smartphone, in your car, or at home. If you start to feel discouraged, pull those messages out and start refueling yourself with the Word.
- Surround yourself with praise and worship music ready to fill the atmosphere. It will dispel discouragement.
- Read a selection of your favorite Psalms that will encourage you and remind you that God promises to deliver you.
- Have a list of scriptures on hand to pull out and meditate on.

I make these things my practice too. As a matter of fact, just the other day, I was cleaning out my office and found so many journals filled with lists I had written. I had lists of scriptures on peace and healing. One was a list about how God wants to bless us with a home. You name it, and I had written a list for it!

I take it to heart when God says, "Present your case to me. Present your arguments. Bring forth your proof" (Isa. 41:21). That is what these lists represent to me.

As I continued searching, I found one list I had forgotten I made. It was one I wrote during those eight years Kevin and I had been trying to have children. I was tempted to be discouraged, but instead I decided to write what I called a "contract" with God! This is what it says:

*Father,*

*Kevin and I are presenting our case before you concerning having children on this first day of April 1996 at 9:30 in the morning. God, our case is built on your Word.*

1. *You said in Genesis 1:28 to be fruitful and multiply. How can I do that unless you help us have children?*
2. *You said in Psalm 112:2 that our children would be mighty in the land. How can these scriptures be fulfilled unless you give us children?*
3. *You said in Psalm 113:9 that you make the barren woman to keep house and to be joyful mother of children. How can I be a joyful mother if we don't have children?*
4. *You said in Luke 1:7 that you take away the reproach of being barren. Father, I don't believe I should live under that reproach.*

*Father, having done all to stand, we present our case to you today with a clear conscience. We have done all that we know to do. We have refused to be discouraged. We have refused to give up. We are looking to you to fulfill your Word.*

*You said, Father, in Luke 18:1 that we should always pray and never give up. Father, I'm like that persistent widow in Luke 18. I will cry out to you day and night until you give us children.*

Kevin and I signed and dated that contract! You have to know what the Bible says about your situation. God's Word is your proof. It is the proof of God's promises to you. Do you have any proof on you? Do you have any evidence that God wants to bless you? Would you be able to argue your case in the court of heaven? If you are going through financial trouble, you ought to be armed with several scriptures that prove God wants to bless you and meet your needs. You ought to be armed and dangerous—fully loaded with God's powerful Word!

You will be greatly encouraged as you meditate on those scriptures over and over until you see them come to pass. And when you do, you will see that God is faithful to deliver you.

## Pray

Many times, we worry for a while first, or we let ourselves get so upset that we forget to pray. We may even talk to person after person about our problem before we ever talk to God about it! I have been guilty of doing that too. It's good to talk to people but not if you're leaving God out. We need to train ourselves to seek and ask God first. That's what Jehoshaphat and David did. We must include God and acknowledge him in all we do. Yes, we are earthly creatures, but we have to remember we have heavenly support!

> *We are earthly creatures with heavenly support!*

Think about that! We have an open invitation from God himself to talk to him about anything, anytime and anywhere! James 1:5 says, "If any of you lacks wisdom, you should ask God, who gives generously to all without finding fault, and it will be given to you." Matthew 7:7 says, "Ask and you will receive, seek and you will find, knock and the door will be open for you." God will tell you things that you need to know when you seek him and ask him.

Years ago, I had a pain in my neck that radiated up my scalp and to my left eye. The pain got worse and worse and began to dominate my life. I went to the doctor, but the doctor couldn't figure out what was causing it. I asked God about it: "God, you know what it is. Would you show me?" I left it at that.

A few days later, I was walking to my car and the answer dropped in my spirit. God reminded me that I clench my teeth at night. I made another doctor's appointment and asked the doctor if that could be causing the problem. He agreed that was the case and explained to me that a nerve had probably become irritated or inflamed because of this. He helped me with the right medication and eventually the pain left. I have been recovered from that issue ever since.

So many times, we forget that we can go "boldly to the throne of grace" in time of need (Heb. 4:16, NKJV). The Bible says that God is "a very present help" in times of trouble (Ps. 46:1, KJV). We need not leave him out when we are facing difficulties, because if we ask him, he will speak to us and even expose the plans of the enemy. As James 4:2 says, "You do not have because you do not ask God."

As I mentioned, don't be afraid to remind God of the promises he's made to you. Remind him of what he has said in his Word. You may be in a financial famine right now or maybe calamity has come to your house. But you have a promise from God. You can have the confidence to know that when you pray, God will deliver you! He said, "Call to Me, and I will answer you, and show you great and mighty things, which you do not know" (Jer. 33:3).

And don't pray puny prayers! "Well, God, I hate to bother you...." "If you *want* to help me...." "If you *can* do anything..." No! Get some backbone. Puny prayers are like a wishbone! Faith-filled prayers are bold and carry the authority you have as one who knows the power of their God. We don't have a puny God! Puny prayers are an insult to him! Puny prayers get puny answers!

> *Don't pray puny prayers! Puny prayers get puny answers!*

Do you remember the leper who came to Jesus in Mark 1? He said, "If you are willing, you can make me clean." Jesus' response was, "I am willing." He touched the man and he was healed. Jesus is saying this to you today, no matter what is coming against you: "Just ask me, because I will say, 'I will.'" God is willing. He will heal you. He will rescue you from your enemies. He will provide for your family. He will give you peace and joy. He is willing.

I'm so glad my parents didn't pray puny prayers when I was born with a crippling disease! If they had not prayed bold prayers, I wouldn't be here today. They said, "Jesus, you are the same yesterday, today, and forever. You can heal our daughter. She's destined to do something for you." They believed God could heal me. They put their faith and trust in God. They asked big, and God completely healed me.

Just as my parents did, David approached God boldly with his inquiry. The Bible tells us that we can do the same. Hebrews 4:16 says, "Let us therefore come *boldly* to the throne of grace, that we may obtain mercy and find grace to help in time of need." Another Bible version says, "Let us then *fearlessly* and *confidently* and *boldly* draw near to the throne of grace" (AMPC, emphasis added). God wants you to have fearless confidence to come into his presence and say, "God, I need this." "God, I have something big but God, I know you're a big God."

Years ago, my mother was bold enough to pray for a swimming pool even when my dad didn't want to spend the money for one.

She began to pray for a pool, and God had a divine connection in store for my mother. She had met a couple whose son had special needs. My mother was so touched by their family that she reached out to them and prayed for their son. She would call to check on them and encourage them. They were so moved by her compassion. What she didn't know was that they owned a construction company that also built pools. One day, the man told my mother, "I want to build you a pool free of charge!"

She was so happy, to say the least! And when the pool was completed, my father started to get in the pool, but my mother wasn't having that! She said, "John, I prayed for this pool that you didn't want, so don't even think about using it!" Of course she was kidding, but she knew God had answered her prayer.

> *Bold prayers get big answers!*

Bold prayers get big answers!

David prayed and asked God some questions: "God, should I pursue my family? Will I overtake the enemy?" And God said, "Pursue and you will recover all! You will succeed!"

## Pursue What You've Lost

We cannot be passive when it comes to the blessings and promises of God. Don't allow Satan to steal your goods. Go after them aggressively. David went after his family and possessions. He had the attitude: "I'm taking back what the enemy stole! I'm not crying over this anymore! I am going to recover all!" That's the attitude you have to have! God will go with you as you resist the enemy and recover all you've lost. He will help you just as he helped David.

My longtime friend Debra George is an evangelist and author.

She also has a major ministry in the inner cities of America, reaching out to those addicted to drugs and alcohol, the homeless, prostitutes, and high-risk children. A few years ago, Debra received an amazing opportunity to speak on an international television program, but at the last minute it was cancelled. It was disappointing to her, but she soon forgot about it.

One day the Lord spoke to her heart and said, "Why don't you ask me to restore that missed opportunity?"

She said, "Lord I didn't even realize that anything had been taken from me."

He replied to her, "Debra, you get so used to things being stolen from you that you don't even realize when you're being stolen from anymore."

She was reminded of the scripture in Joel 2:25 that says, "I will give back to you what you lost" (NLT). She began to ask God to restore not only that missed opportunity but other things that came to her mind as she meditated on this challenge God had placed before her.

Within two weeks, not only had God restored the missed opportunity, but also he opened a greater television opportunity for her as well! As he did for Debra and David, God desires to restore what the enemy has stolen from you too.

The Bible says that David recovered all he had lost, and there was nothing lacking, small or great, sons or daughters. Everything that was taken was recovered—and even what was not taken! David and his men plundered the enemy's camp and came home with more than they'd lost! Does this sound familiar? There seems to be a pattern here. Think back to the end result of Jehoshaphat's victory.

The message here is that God will help you recover what you lost—and more! God is all about more!

## Three Days from Victory

David's recovery at Ziklag will put the fight back in you, but there's something even more amazing about this story. The Bible tells us that it was just three days after David's abundant recovery at Ziklag that Saul died and he was appointed king of Israel. Just three days!

Think about this: In his darkest hour, David was only three days away from fulfilling his destiny! No more hiding from the enemy! Instead, he was living in a palace as the reigning king!

All I can say is this: You may be just three days from your promise!

I love what Amos 9:13–15 says: "'Yes indeed, it won't be long now.'... 'Things are going to happen so fast your head will swim, one thing fast on the heels of the other. You won't be able to keep up. Everything will be happening at once—and everywhere you look, blessings! Blessings like wine pouring off the mountains and hills. I'll make everything right again'" (THE MESSAGE). Don't you just love that!

Your victory is around the corner! Be encouraged today! This is not the time to give up but to press in and recover all!

---

### PRACTICAL APPLICATION

*Encouraging thoughts and scriptures to meditate on:*

- I will not give in to pity and blame. I recognize Satan is my real enemy, and I have authority over him. First Peter 5:8–9 says, "Be alert and of sober mind. Your enemy the devil prowls around like a roaring lion looking for someone to devour. Resist him standing firm in the faith."

Luke 10:19: "I have given you authority over all the power of the enemy and nothing shall by any means hurt you."

James 4:7: "Resist the devil, and he will flee from you."

- God is always willing to help me. Mark 1:40–42 says, "A man with leprosy came and knelt in front of Jesus, begging to be healed. 'If you are willing, you can heal me and make me clean,' he said. Moved with compassion, Jesus reached out and touched him. 'I am willing,' he said. 'Be healed!' Instantly the leprosy disappeared, and the man was healed."

- God will help me recover what I lost—and more! My victory is just around the corner! First Samuel 30:8 says, "So David inquired of the Lord…And He answered him, 'Pursue, for you shall surely overtake them and without fail recover all'" (NKJV).

### Practical steps you can take:

- I will make it my new default to pray and seek God first.

- I will begin to encourage myself when I recognize the first onset of discouragement.

- I will pray bold prayers because I serve a great God.

# 4

# Do It Right—No More Shortcuts

⌘

*You have made your way around this hill country long enough;*
*now turn north.*

—Deuteronomy 2:3

After waiting so long—according to your timing, at least—you may begin to wonder when the breakthrough, the answer, or the healing will come. Maybe you feel like you've prayed, praised, and believed as much as you could and still nothing is happening, and you're getting tired. Maybe you are crying out, "God, I've done everything I know to do! Why aren't things changing? I need some help here! I'm drowning!" It seems we have done all the right things, but nothing has changed. Is this where you are today? If so, I want to help relieve some of your frustration.

We have to realize that most miracles usually don't happen instantly or overnight. You have to continue to keep your trust and faith in God right now in the process. There is no other way around it. The Bible says that "everyone who believes in him will never be disappointed" (Rom. 10:11, TPT). God will not disappoint you so don't give up now! Galatians 6:9 says, "Let us not become weary in doing good, for at the proper time we will reap a harvest if we do not give up."

This is the time to continue to persevere. You've come this far. Don't get tired now. Don't give up and try to do it your own way. Don't give up on holding out for the right one and marry the wrong person. Trust God when he says, "If you are willing and obedient, you shall eat the good of the land" (Isa. 1:19). In the waiting time, we may be tempted to compromise, to take a shortcut, but you will not reap God's best when you try to cut corners. You don't escape the opportunities to learn and grow. You will just cycle round and round the mountain until you get it.

I've been in the ministry for a long time, and I minister to people who often want to take the easy way out of their problems. I get it. In fact, I used to be one of those people! But I've learned that there are no shortcuts to victory. There are no shortcuts when it comes to obeying God and his Word.

We all like a quick fix. It's our human nature to want it done and want it done now! So, we look for the shortcut, the faster route. Like when I'm in rush-hour traffic, I know exactly which shortcuts to take that will get me to where I am going faster. The problem is, when it comes to our everyday life situations, shortcuts don't always work like they do on the road.

I remember my dad telling the story about a time he tried to take a shortcut when he was a little boy working on the family cotton farm in Paris, Texas. His father had given him a bucket of seeds to plant down several rows, but being a little boy, Daddy got tired of that fast. He looked down those rows that seemed too long for his little legs to walk down and decided it would take him forever to complete the task! There must be a faster way.

Instead of doing it how his father instructed him, he dumped all of the seeds in one hole, covered them up, and dusted off his hands. "No one will ever know I did that," he thought. But when the crops began to grow and harvest time came, there was this very obvious, very ugly tangled-up mess of cotton all together in one place!

So many times, in our own lives, we think we can take a shortcut. Things get hard and seem to be going on a little bit too long for our comfort. We participate in a little disobedience here and there. We may ignore the voice of reason or wise counsel. And maybe we compromise the Word of God, thinking God couldn't have meant it to be this hard for this long. We rationalize our actions, telling ourselves that our little shortcut or quick fix doesn't hurt anything. But those shortcuts actually do show up, just as they did in my father's story. They are noticeable. And they can prolong our situation and problems, creating a whole tangled-up mess that could make your situation worse.

If you are like me, you may have had experiences that prove that instant relief doesn't always mean permanent relief. Sometimes trying to take the easy route prolongs our misery. I want to see an end to the problem right now just like you do. But I have learned that, as much as I want to see a quick end to my pain or problem, it's not always going to happen that way. We can complain and cry and worry and try to rush God, but doing that doesn't help anything! The process is there for a reason, and we can't rush it.

## Don't Rush the Process

God is great, and he does great and supernatural things. We've heard stories of people receiving instant miracles from the Bible, and we even hear stories like this in our everyday lives, but things don't often happen that way. Most of the time, we have to go through the process. And there's no rushing the process. I try to comfort and encourage myself in this. I remind myself that God has me covered and I don't have to rush him or worry about how things will turn out. He promised that he would cause all things to work together for my good because I love him. (See Romans 8:28.) Then there are other times, I get frustrated and do my own thing. Can you relate?

Not long ago, for instance, I had a pity party. I hadn't had one in a long time, and it was sort of nice! I had come to a point where I was just fed up with some of the things I was going through at the time. I was tired and determined to be mad. So, I sat down in my chair and started thinking about everything. One thing topped the other, and the aggravation and frustration rose.

Unaware of the party in progress, Kevin, who had been working outside, came in the house. After looking at me for a moment just kind of sitting there in that chair, he asked, "What are you doing?"

"I'm being mad!" I said.

"What are you mad at?"

"Everything!" I said, as if everything in my life *was* really bad! A pity party will do this to you. It will give the enemy room to magnify our problems and make us feel that everything in our lives is terrible.

Kevin was really good to try to encourage me. He told me not to be mad and know who the real enemy is.

I said, "Okay, I know you're right, but right now, I want to be mad!"

Leaving me to it, Kevin went on to finish what he was doing. I stayed at my party for another hour or so before I got up and decided to go on with my life. Ultimately, I knew that the bottom line was and still is that God will take care of everything. He has me covered. Being mad didn't help anything really. I probably just needed to process my emotions and let out some frustration. But when it was all said and done, none of it helped the process. As a matter of fact, whenever I do try to rush the process or get frustrated and try to do my own thing, I always end up back at square one, which is trusting God like I should have done all along, realizing he knew what he was doing.

I know you thought I was more spiritual than that, but sometimes I have to learn it the hard way too!

Satan will always try to move us away from faith and trust, tempting us to believe that that the grass is greener on the other side. He's done this since the beginning, when he lied to Adam and Eve in the Garden of Eden. They had everything they could ever ask for or dream of. God even walked and talked with them. But, thief that he is, Satan came in to steal their place with God and to plant ideas in their minds about all they were missing out on. He came in to convince them that, even in this place of abundance, they were lacking.

Genesis 3:1 says, "The serpent was the shrewdest of all the wild animals the Lord God had made. One day he asked the woman, 'Did God really say you must not eat the fruit from any of the trees in the garden?'" (NLT).

Notice that, from the start, Satan twisted the Word of God. He misquoted what God said, but Eve corrected him. She said, "Of course we may eat fruit from the trees in the garden.... It's only the fruit from the tree in the middle of the garden that we are not allowed to eat. God said, 'You must not eat it or even touch it; if you do, you will die'" (v. 2, NLT). She did well at first.

Still, Satan went on twisting and contradicting God's words: "You won't die!" (v. 4, NLT), he said. Then he painted a pretty picture that got her to believe him: "God knows that your eyes will be opened as soon as you eat it, and you will be like God, knowing both good and evil" (v. 5, NLT).

Oh, Eve liked that idea! She was convinced. Satan's rationale appeals to her flesh and ego, and she began to see that:

> *The tree was beautiful and its fruit looked delicious, and she wanted the wisdom it would give her. So she took some of the fruit and ate it. Then she gave some to her husband, who was with her, and he ate it, too. At that moment, their eyes were opened, and they suddenly felt shame at their nakedness. So they sewed fig leaves together to cover themselves.* (vv. 6–7)

We know the rest of the story. We are living the outcome. The Bible says, "Their eyes were open" (v. 7), and they realized God was right all along.

Settle this truth in your mind: God is right all the time. Don't let Satan come in and lie to you. Don't let him paint a pretty picture that contradicts the Word of God. Stop and declare this truth aloud right now. Say, "God, you are right all the time!"

> God is right all the time.

## Do It Right the First Time

One Christmas season, our daughter Caroline and I were putting lights on our Christmas tree. We had so many strings of lights that we decided to put all of them on the tree to make it really bright. When we got to the top third of the tree, however, we realized that we didn't really have enough lights. Since we did not want to go back to the store and buy more lights, we decided we would stretch them to make it work.

Once all the lights were on the tree, we felt like we had accomplished exactly what we'd set out to do—until we stood back to see how it looked. As you can imagine, it looked like we had taken a shortcut. The bottom of the tree was well lit, but the top wasn't. It looked sad. And even though we thought we'd come up with a good plan to avoid restringing all the lights, it turned out that we still had to take the top lights off the tree, go back to the store, get more lights, and do it right the second time around. Our shortcut only prolonged the process.

> *Instead of learning it the hard way, let's do it right the first time!*

This reminds me about how the Israelites never entered into their Promised Land because they always wanted the easy way out. They wanted to do it their way. All along, the wilderness was supposed to have been just temporary. It was their pathway to their Promised Land. But instead of trusting God, they complained and compromised time after time. They actually prolonged their stay in the wilderness for forty years, when all along God had wanted them to move forward. Studies show us that it could have been an eleven-day trip!

You know, the whole reason I am writing this book and sharing these stories with you is because I want to see you move forward into your Promised Land. There is so much God has for you if you will hold on, don't lose heart, and keep doing the right thing. If you keep taking shortcuts—trying to get around the path God has laid out for you—you will prolong the process and your misery.

The issue here is not that God won't give us chance after chance. We know from the Israelites' wilderness experience that God will allow you to circle the mountain over and over again. Yes, God will always give us another chance. Thank God for his mercy! The issue is whether you are going to do what you need to do—the right thing—to keep yourself from unnecessary hardship!

I heard someone say once, "You either do it the hard way first and your life is easier. Or, you do it the easy way first and your life is harder." Nothing worth having comes easy. It takes determination, courage, and waiting on God as he brings you closer to your answer. So whatever you do, don't throw in the towel! Don't circle that mountain or go through the desert again. Take God's Word as full truth. He knows what he's talking about. What you are waiting for is on the way!

## Pass the Obedience Test

In order to keep from compromising your position when things get tough, you must obey God fully.

Sometimes it is hard to obey God, not because we don't want to, but because it doesn't seem fair or right when we're being mistreated. It doesn't seem fair that we still have to do what's right when other people are doing wrong. When people are saying things about you or doing evil things against you, you don't necessarily have a desire to obey the Word and pray for them and bless them. But obedience brings great blessings into your life. Forgiving your enemies and praying for them helps you stay free from anger and bitterness. It softens your heart and keeps those people from controlling your life.

It is better for us to obey God first and foremost. Shortcuts do not work here, because if we don't pass the obedience test the first time, we have to start over and take the test again! The sooner we align with God and how he wants us to respond to our enemies, the sooner we walk in victory and experience the blessings that come from obedience. God rewards those who obey him.

Acts 5:29 says, "We ought to obey God rather than men" (NKJV). I like to say it this way. We must obey God rather than:

- The voice of people
- Our feelings
- Our emotions
- The voice of Satan
- The voice of compromise

Obedience is a step of faith. Sometimes it means stepping out into the unknown. One of my assignments in writing this book is to help you grow in your faith. God wants you to develop an unshakeable confidence in him. Hebrews 11:6 says, "And without faith it is impossible to please God, because anyone who comes to Him must believe that He exists and that He rewards those who earnestly seek Him."

God works by faith, and he rewards your faith. Obedience is a demonstration of faith. It demonstrates that you believe God will do what he said he would do. Doing what God says demonstrates that you trust him even when you don't understand him, and that you have an unshakeable confidence in your heavenly Father!

I remember hearing the story of Charles Blondin, the famous tightrope walker. He made a name for himself by walking across very high and dangerous places like the Grand Canyon and Niagara Falls. Crowds of people would come and watch his death-defying feats. They were mesmerized and amazed by his stunts. One time he attempted what seemed like a very unstable walk across Niagara Falls and the crowd let out a big sigh of relief, cheers, and applause when he finished. Then he proceeded to walk across it several more times, even stopping to sit in a chair in the middle. Clearly, he was a master acrobat.

Before his final trip across, and after it seemed he had gained the audience's trust, he asked for a volunteer to let him push them across the falls in a wheelbarrow. They had come to see how capable he was at getting himself back and forth on the narrow line. But how far did that trust go if it involved their own lives? No one volunteered!

As the story goes, his manager finally jumped in the wheelbarrow and he took him safely across.[1]

You see, obedience is faith in action, because "faith without works is dead" (James 2:26). It is jumping in God's wheelbarrow and saying, "God, I trust you." Obeying God is where you take yourself out of your own care and put yourself in the care of your heavenly Father. Many times—though we may not want to admit it—it can feel like such a stretch to put your whole life in God's hands, but that is exactly what we must do. It doesn't always feel good or even safe, but obeying God is for our good. Sometimes we don't understand why God is asking us to do a certain thing. But the more you obey, the easier it becomes and the more you believe God is for you, working everything out for your good.

> *Everything God asks you to do will ultimately work out for YOUR GOOD and HIS PURPOSES.*

When you obey God, you will have God's best! You will experience victory! First Corinthians 2:9 says, "No eye has seen, no ear has heard, and no mind has imagined what God has prepared for those who love Him." I love the Message translation of Jeremiah 29:11–14:

---

[1] "Charles Blondin: Real Trust Is Getting in the Wheelbarrow," Histagory.com, January 7, 2017, https://www.histagory.com/single-post/2017/01/09/Charles-Blondin-Real-Trust-is-Getting-in-the-Wheelbarrow.

*[God says,] I know what I'm doing. I have it all planned out—plans to take care of you, not abandon you, plans to give you the future you hoped for. When you call on Me, when you come and pray to Me, I'll listen. When you come looking for Me, you'll find Me. Yes, when you get serious about finding Me and want it more than anything else, I'll make sure you won't be disappointed. I'll turn things around for you. (emphasis added)*

Let these verses encourage you, because when you get serious and stop taking shortcuts, you will not be disappointed. God will turn things around for you, just as he did for the people of Israel when he delivered them out of their captivity.

The psalmist wrote about it in Psalm 126. Not only was it a testimony of what God did for the Israelites, but it is also a picture of what God wants to do for you:

*When the Lord brought back his exiles to Jerusalem, it was like a dream! We were filled with laughter, and we sang for joy. And the other nations said, "What amazing things the Lord has done for them." Yes, the Lord has done amazing things for us! What joy! Restore our fortunes, Lord, as streams renew the desert. Those who plant in tears will harvest with shouts of joy. They weep as they go to plant their seed, but they sing as they return with the harvest. (emphasis added)*

Do you see the pattern? You may be in tears today, but when YOU OBEY GOD, he will bring laughter and joy into your life. He will do amazing things in your life!

## Stay the Course

I know your circumstances aren't easy and there are times when it seems like the bad days outweigh the good, but stay the course. Refuse to get off track, turning neither to the left nor to the right. Be faithful day after day. And when you mess up, be faithful to repent, ask God to forgive you, and get right back on track. When the battle gets long and you are growing weary, remind yourself of these three things:

1. I will stay the course because God's path is the best path.
2. Staying the course is MY BEST OPTION.
3. Staying the course is the path to complete freedom and victory.

When you are trusting God for a financial breakthrough and it seems like it will never come, stay the course! When healing seems to evade you, stay the course! When it looks like the enemy has the upper hand in your life, stay the course.

Keep reading the Word. Keep praying. Keep attending church and staying connected to faith-filled people. Keep knocking, seeking, and asking. Keep the right attitude. Keep sowing and being generous. Keep a guard over your mouth and the things you say. Stay the course.

Don't allow people to talk you out of doing the right thing. Don't give up and compromise. Keep your eyes on Jesus. He is the captain of your salvation who will lead you into victory. He is your anchor in the storms of life. He is your peace in the midst of your chaos! He is your great physician and healer. He is your keeper and sustainer. He is your restorer who will recover *all* for you and give you a double portion of joy! He is your wisdom and your hiding place. He will protect you from trouble and surround you with songs of deliverance. He is your shepherd who will lead you beside still waters and into paths of righteousness.

You are anointed to keep going. Psalm 23:5 says that God will anoint your head with oil so that you can keep going. He will prepare a table for you in the presence of your enemies. Shortcuts lead to unnecessary detours and heartache. They compromise your end result. You miss out on seeing the saving and delivering power of God on full display when you take the shortcut or cheat the process. God fights your battles for you when you do things the right way—no shortcuts.

God has extraordinary things in store for you, so stay the course and do it right the first time! Stay the course, because it is worth it. Stay the course, and know your victory is on the way!

## PRACTICAL APPLICATION

*Encouraging thoughts and scriptures to meditate on:*

- God's ways and timing will bring about his best for my life. Galatians 6:9 says, "Let us not become weary in doing good, for at the proper time we will reap a harvest if we do not give up."

- Obeying God fully will bring rewards and blessing in my life. Isaiah 1:19 says, "If you are willing and obedient, you will eat the good of the land."

- Staying the course God has laid out for me is my best option. He has ordered my steps. Psalm 37:23 says, "The steps of a good man are ordered by the LORD, and He delights in his way" (NKJV).

### *Practical steps you can take:*

- I will not compromise or take shortcuts because my victory is coming.

- I will do things right the first time by waiting on God and trusting his wisdom.

- I will trust God to turn my sorrow into joy and bring me to victory!

# 5

# Press Through Until You Break Through

∽

*The Lord has broken through my enemies before me, like the bursting out of great waters. So he called the name of that place Baal-perazim [Lord of breaking through].*

—2 Samuel 5:20, AMP

Have you noticed how sometimes the opposition is stronger than other times? Sometimes it's circumstances and people, but other times it's spiritual opposition. Ephesians 6 says that "we wrestle not against flesh and blood but against principalities and powers of this dark world and against the spiritual forces of evil in the heavenly realm. Therefore put on the full armor of God and take your stand against the schemes of the enemy."

About three years ago, I had been praying about some specific things for a while, asking God to speak to me and show me why I felt opposition spiritually, when I preached and at other times. One day, I had come to church a little heavyhearted. Initially, I didn't feel like getting dressed up or going to church, but I made myself go anyway. It's always a good decision to go to church even when you don't feel like it! It makes such a difference when we get in the presence of God. Where he is, his anointing is also there. It's good to come together and worship his holy and mighty name. It really does make such a difference. It made a difference for me that day, because while I was worshipping, God dropped these words in my spirit: "Lisa, keep pressing through and you will get your breakthrough."

Oh, how I needed to hear that! God spoke that word to me in such a way that I knew exactly what he was saying, and so I say it to you right now: Your answer is coming, but you have to do something.

We've discussed doing it right the first time, obeying God, and staying the course. We've also discussed recognizing the real enemy, encouraging yourself, and going to God in prayer first. While all this remains true and necessary, God is also saying something more about the force and energy you put behind these actions as you pursue the things he has for you. You must press through all the opposition and all the negative emotions, and you will break through to the other side. You will see God's promises to you fulfilled!

About one year after God spoke that word to me, something lifted off of me and I stepped into a freedom like never before! I knew that what I had felt was a spiritual assignment from Satan, but as I continued to press through the opposition, my breakthrough came.

The word *press* means "to steadily apply weight or force; to move by force in a certain direction or into a certain position."[2] God wants you to press in and keep moving forward so that you get into your new position. Through the opposition you are facing, God is

---

[2] Dictionary.com, s.v. "press," https://www.dictionary.com/browse/press?s=t.

turning your situation for good. He will use what the enemy tried to stop you with to move you forward into something new. I sense it by the Holy Spirit! He has a new place and season for you. It will be a season of breakthrough.

I think about the woman with the issue of blood in Mark 5. She was desperate to get to Jesus. She had been sick and bleeding for twelve long years. She spent all she had on doctors and they couldn't help her. Instead she became worse. Then she heard about Jesus, the miracle-worker who was coming to town. She said, "If I can just touch his garment, I know I will be made whole."

To get to her breakthrough, her healing, she had to press through the throngs of people. She was considered unclean because of her sickness and I can imagine that she received some looks and criticism, but she didn't give up. She came up behind Jesus and touched his garment, and at that moment she was healed!

Jesus said, "Who touched me?"

Even though she was afraid and trembling, she fell down before Jesus and told him the story. Then he said to her, "Daughter, your faith [your personal trust and confidence in me] has restored you to health; go in peace and be [permanently] healed from your suffering." (See Mark 5:24–34.)

God is going to do some permanent healing in your life—spiritual healing, emotional or physical healing. He is saying to you today, "Daughter/son, your faith, your personal trust, and confidence in me has restored you. Now go in peace, and be permanently healed from your suffering."

This is the season when you are going to get free from some things. You are going to experience permanent healing, deliverance, and restitution. What you've been waiting for is coming, but you must press through!

The apostle Paul had to do the same. He said, "I press on to take hold of that which Christ Jesus took hold of me....I press toward the goal" (Phil. 3:13–14). If you go back and read through Paul's story, you will see how everything in the world came against him, and yet he pressed on. He fulfilled his destiny. He pressed. The woman with the issue of blood pressed.

Pressing is the action we must take. It is an act of faith. If we don't act, we will remain in the same place and position. Our act of faith activates our breakthrough. It is what God does for us in response to our pressing. In 2 Samuel 5:20 we find the story of David defeating the Philistines in the Valley of Rephaim. After the victory, David named that place Baal Perazim because he said, "The Lord has broken out against my enemies before me." *Baal Perazim* literally means "Lord of the breakthroughs."[3] We serve a God who is the Lord of the breakthrough! What we cannot break through, he can!

> *You serve a God who is the Lord of the breakthrough! What you cannot break through, he can!*

We must press through even though it seems like we aren't getting anywhere, not gaining any ground. Sometimes it seems like the opposition is even pushing us backward. The woman with the issue of blood shows us how to press through, but so does Jesus. He spent forty days in the wilderness for a time of prayer and fasting, but during this time he faced the attack of the enemy. Satan came to tempt him over and over again. Every time he threw a lie at Jesus, Jesus pressed back with the truth of the Word of God. Jesus refused to compromise in any way, answering Satan three times with a resounding declaration, "Satan, it is written in God's Word."

---

[3] *Holman Bible Dictionary*, s.v. "*Baal-Perazim*," StudyLight.org, https://www.studylight.org/dictionaries/hbd/b/baal-perazim.html.

Jesus pressed through the time of temptation until Satan left his presence. In the same way, Satan will come to tempt and discourage you, but you can resist him with the Word and in the name of Jesus. You have that authority!

My father, Pastor John Osteen, is in heaven now, but he once told the story of a significant dream he had from God. There was a time when he was in his forties when he had lost all motivation to preach. Actually, he said he felt like he was having a nervous breakdown. He was under tremendous stress and could not figure out how he'd arrived at this place in his life. He had always been energetic and could preach at the drop of a hat! But at this time, he didn't feel like himself, and he earnestly prayed and asked God to show him what he needed to do. That's when God spoke to my dad through a dream.

In the dream, my father was in a small room with another man. They were both sitting in chairs. The other man decided he wanted out of the room, but he couldn't get the door open. He pushed and pulled, kicked on the door, and finally began to scream, "Let me out of here!" To his disappointment, no one came and he gave up, sinking to the floor in defeat.

When this happened, my father got up out of his chair, marched with authority to the door and declared, "I will walk out of here in the name of Jesus!" He then opened the door and walked out.

My dad woke up immediately and God impressed upon his spirit these words: "Son, you can walk out of your situation in the authority I have given you."

From that time forward, my father refused to give up, pressed through and got his breakthrough into complete freedom and healing.

The temptation is to stop and say, "It's too much. It's too hard. It's too big. I can't do it." But you can press through with the help of the Holy Spirit, and you *must* press through. Believe me, I know sometimes the pressure is so heavy and intense. I feel it too, but you must push back. You must take action.

Nehemiah is another example of what it looks like to press through when the opposition is relentless. Nehemiah was an Israelite captive in Babylon who served as the king's cupbearer. God used him to rebuild the wall around the city of Jerusalem in fifty-two days—a feat in itself. What's more interesting is that he wasn't a carpenter or builder. He was an ordinary person like you and me—with a passion to do something for God.

## Life in Ruins

> *In the month of Kislev in the twentieth year, while I was in the citadel of Susa, Hanani, one of my brothers, came from Judah with some other men, and I questioned them about the Jewish remnant that had survived the exile, and also about Jerusalem. They said, "Those who survived the exile are in great trouble and disgrace. The wall of Jerusalem is broken down, and its gates have been burned with fire." When I heard these things, I sat down and wept. For some days I mourned and fasted and prayed before the God of heaven. (Nehemiah 1:1–4, emphasis added)*

Jerusalem was in ruins because the king of Babylon attacked the city and burned the temple and palaces. His armies broke down the walls and virtually destroyed everything of value. When Nehemiah found out about the situation, it touched his heart, and passion arose within him to see Jerusalem return to its previous splendor. So he purposed in his heart to help rebuild Jerusalem.

As you read the passage above, was there anything in your own situation that has left you feeling like your life is in ruins? Are you feeling like you are in "great trouble and disgrace"? Like the walls to your heart have been broken down? Be comforted in knowing that, like Jerusalem, God wants to pick up the pieces and rebuild your life. The master builder and carpenter did not forget about Jerusalem and he has not forgotten about you! Let's see how he remembers and restores.

The first action Nehemiah took toward seeing his dream fulfilled was pray. As I studied the Book of Nehemiah, I noticed that all through it, prayer is always shown as his default. He prayed for favor with the king because he wanted time off to do the job. When he eventually approached the king, he was so afraid, but he did it anyway.

And he didn't just ask for a little time off; he asked big! He didn't pray any puny prayers. He asked for lumber, transportation, and letters of approval so that people would know he had the king's permission. The king granted all of his requests! His big prayers got big answers. He pressed through the fear and got his breakthrough.

It should have been all good from there, right? Nehemiah got all the yesses it seemed he needed. He was ready to begin work. But this next level came with opposition. Sanballat, Tobiah, and Geshem were members of neighboring enemy nations and they were not happy about the work Nehemiah was getting ready to do. They didn't like the fact that someone was promoting the welfare of Israel.

When you set out to do the will of God, the enemy is not going to sit around and watch you. This is the time you have to press through with your faith, prayer, and perseverance. In Nehemiah's experience, three ways to do this rise to the surface.

*1. Ignore the persecution and criticism (Neh. 2:10, 19; 4:1–3).*

The Bible says that three men—Sanballat, Tobiah, and Geshem—actually ridiculed and mocked Nehemiah and the Israelites, saying things like: "What are you feeble Jews doing?" "You are just rebelling against the king!" "Do you think you really are going to restore your wall?" "If even a fox climbed up your wall, it would break down."

They were trying to make Nehemiah doubt his work and his own calling. The enemy executes this same plan in your life. He tries to make you doubt your dreams, doubt God and even yourself to heap insecurity upon you. If that is happening to you, then you must be a real threat to the enemy! You must have a great calling on your life!

Second Timothy 3:12 says, "Everyone who wants to live a godly life in Christ Jesus will be persecuted." Persecution comes with the territory and that's why you can't be faint-hearted! You have to turn a deaf ear to the naysayers!

With the king's permission, Nehemiah could have gone back to appeal to the king to back him up against the men's taunting and accusations, but he didn't. He did two very important things.

First, he didn't answer his accusers. Instead, he appealed to God in prayer. Nehemiah recognized that he was in a spiritual battle, and he knew how to win it. He knew where his strength and help came from. Psalm 121:1 says, "I will lift up my eyes to the hills—where does my help come from? My help comes from the Lord, the Maker of heaven and earth."

It's tempting to talk about what people are saying when you are being ridiculed. It's really tempting to try to answer your accusers, but that's not how you get your breakthrough. You get your breakthrough by pressing through in prayer. Earlier we discussed making prayer your default. As soon as you feel opposition or trouble, run to God's throne, where you will find help in your time of need.

The second thing Nehemiah did was to keep on working. He didn't let anything stop him. He and the men kept building—pressing through the criticism, distraction, and persecution. Faith must have tenacity—a bulldog determination!

First Corinthians 15:58 says, "Therefore, my beloved brethren, be steadfast, immovable, always abounding in the work of the Lord, knowing that your labor is not in vain in the Lord" (NKJV). You have to be unmovable when it comes to the things of God and press through the persecution! Here's the next thing we can learn from Nehemiah:

*2. You have to press through discouragement (Neh. 4:7–23).*

When Nehemiah's enemies couldn't get him with ridicule, they plotted to attack and kill Nehemiah and the Israelites. The Israelites became discouraged. They started looking at all the rubble around them and thinking about the threats of the enemy. They complained to Nehemiah, "We are tired and worn out! There is so much rubble we don't see how we can rebuild the wall" (Neh. 4:10).

Nehemiah rallied them together for prayer again. It was always his default. He said to them, "Don't focus your eyes on the rubble and the enemy." He challenged them to stay focused on the mission. He said, "Don't be afraid of the enemy! Remember the Lord, who is great and glorious, and fight for your brothers, your sons, your daughters, your wives, and your homes!" (v. 14). Building that wall represented safety and protection. Back in Nehemiah's time, walls were also a place where cities would hold court, hear cases, make judgments, and pass legislation. A strong wall meant a strong city, so the task of rebuilding Jerusalem's wall was an urgent and necessary one. Their homes and family life were at stake. What's at stake if you don't keep pressing? Remember who or what are you fighting for and refuse to give up!

Next, something very interesting happened. God frustrated the plans of the enemy and the Israelites returned to work. Just like that, God moved supernaturally when Nehemiah prayed. He strengthened the men to continue the rebuilding of the wall. The Bible tells us that when the men returned to work, they held a weapon in one hand and worked with the other hand (vv. 17–18). This is a picture of what we have to do. We keep our Sword of the Spirit—the Word of God—in one hand and keep moving forward, keep building toward our dreams, keep waiting for the vision, keep believing the promises of God, because they will not tarry. They will surely come to pass. It's on the way. Keep declaring the Word of God and refuse to stop! God will frustrate the plans of your enemy!

### 3. Press through the temptation to compromise (Neh. 6:1–14).

The third thing we learn from Nehemiah's example is not to settle for less than God's best. That is exactly what compromise is. It's interesting to me that the enemy tempted Nehemiah to compromise at the very end of the project when he only had the gates to hang in order to complete the walls.

Many times, the greatest opportunity to compromise comes just before the victory. We saw this in David's story. His appointment to being king of Israel was just three days after his victory at Ziklag. What would have happened if he did not have the courage to obey God, to press through his enormous grief to pursue the enemy, and recover all that had been stolen? What would have happened if David had not held his ground? What might he have compromised?

> *Many times, the greatest opportunity to compromise comes just before the victory.*

The challenge here is to be on your guard. Be discerning and aware of the schemes of the enemy. Stick to it through the very end. Do not ease up just before the battle is over or the race has been won. Have you ever seen those track and field events where the runner has held the lead the whole race only to lose at the finish line? They are confident that they've got the race in the bag, and next thing you know a runner from second or third place picks up the pace and secures the victory. Don't be like this. Be like Nehemiah who held it together and pressed through till the very end. Let's see how he did it.

The work was just about complete when Sanballat, Tobiah, and Geshem sent a message to Nehemiah that they wanted to meet with him. They wanted to make a deal with him—and Nehemiah wouldn't have anything to do with it. They kept coming back and pressed him to meet with them four different times.

That's how temptation works. Satan will try to wear you down. He will pressure you and pressure you to see if you will give in.

Nehemiah's answer every time was, "No! Why should I stop the work of the Lord to meet with you?" That can preach! The enemy wants to stop you, but I love Nehemiah's fortitude and courage. He refused to compromise, and he began to pray, "Lord, strengthen my hands!" The Bible says that Nehemiah finished the wall. It was a great victory for the people of Israel. They had pressed through persecution, criticism, discouragement, and the temptation to compromise, and they got their breakthrough!

Sometimes the temptation we feel to quit, to sin, or to compromise—to take the shortcut or easy way—is so strong, but you have to be like Nehemiah and say, "No! Lord, strengthen my hands!" Refuse to make a deal with the enemy! The Holy Spirit will come to your aid when you are in need. All you have to do is call on God. Psalm 60:12 says, "With God we will gain the victory, and he will trample down our enemies."

When you do it God's way, you get his results—which are exceedingly abundantly above all that you could ask or think (Eph. 3:20).

When you do it your way, you get your results. Do it God's way and get his results.

Don't you get frustrated when your children will not listen to you? You know what's right for them, but they just won't listen to you! Sometimes you have to calm yourself down and remember that the frontal cortex of their brain isn't fully developed yet. They think they know what is best, and sometimes curiosity gets the best of them.

When our daughter Caroline was little, all you had to do was tell her not to do something and she would do it! The thing she was not supposed to do became a challenge to her.

We'd say, "Caroline, don't walk on that little brick wall again." Well, she did it and fell and the sprinkler head scraped her back and she still has the scar today.

"Caroline, don't touch the mousetrap because it will hurt you." Ten minutes later, we'd hear her scream. She had gotten a chair, pulled it up to the drawer, and found that mousetrap—and there it was on her hand.

"Caroline," I'd say, "don't ever touch my curling irons because they will burn you." You know the rest of the story. I even kept them hidden, but that didn't stop her. So she has a big burn scar on her arm.

At some point Caroline finally realized that we were only trying to protect her and that we knew what was best for her.

If this is true for what we wanted and knew for Caroline, and what you know and would desire for your own children, how much more does God know and want what is best for you? When you live a life of no compromise, you are choosing God's highest and best for your life.

The Bible teaches us to give 100 percent to the Lord. We need to be all in—not one foot in the kingdom of God and one foot in the world. I know it takes a new Christian time to learn the Word and do what pleases God, but you should not remain a baby Christian. We need to grow up spiritually!

Romans 12:1–2 says:

> And so, dear brothers and sisters, I plead with you to give your bodies to God because of all he has done for you. Let them be a living and holy sacrifice—the kind he will find acceptable. This is truly the way to worship him. Don't copy the behavior and customs of this world, but let God transform you into a new person by changing the way you think. Then you will learn to know God's will for you, which is good and pleasing and perfect. (NLT)

The Bible also teaches us to separate ourselves from the world. We may live in the world, but we are not of the world. We must live to obey God, his Word, and his will for our lives. It's when you surrender yourself fully to God that you begin to be transformed in every area of your life and you begin to understand his will for your life.

How our parents raised us may seem old-fashioned to some,

but the principles are still relevant for today. From the Bible, our parents taught us to:

- Guard what we listen to and what we watch. My dad would say, "If you put trash in, then trash comes out."
- Guard who we run around with because they will rub off on you.
- Abstain from even the appearance of evil.

I like good music, but some of the music today has gone to an all new low. If you listen to music that has sexual innuendos and curse words all through it, then you're going to be tempted in those areas.

I've found that I have to guard my mind, my spirit, and the anointing upon my life. I want worship songs coming up out of my spirit. I want my mind to be on the things of God. You and I have enough to battle with, and we don't need to make it worse!

God said, "Be holy as I am holy." We are to live a life of purity—a life free from sexual immorality. Sexual purity that pleases God is between a husband and wife, not a boyfriend and girlfriend or a casual date. You are the temple of the Holy Spirit, and God wants to protect you in your body, mind, and emotions. He wants you free from unnecessary baggage in your life. (See 1 Peter 1:16.)

If this has been your lifestyle, it's time to grow up! I'm not here to shame or condemn you in any way; I am here to help you get on the best path for your life, where you will not compromise the blessing, provision, and protection of God! I desire to see you thriving in every area of your life.

Ephesians 4:29 says, "Don't use foul or abusive language. Let everything you say be good and helpful, so that your words will be an encouragement to those who hear them. And do not bring sorrow to God's Holy Spirit by the way you live." Don't grieve the Holy Spirit by the way you live. Let your words be kind and encouraging. Live a life of integrity and character. Be truthful!

I know you are thinking: "I thought we were talking about pressing through to your breakthrough." We are! I want to share the truth with you about what it means to press, to stay the course, to not lay down and become a victim of the enemy.

A no-compromise life is a separated and holy life, a life that is pleasing to God. He calls us to a higher standard and yet blesses us beyond measure.

What we have uncovered in this chapter with the help of Nehemiah are some of the things that will help you press through to your breakthrough. You will have to press through persecution, discouragement, and, when the victory or the finish line is in sight, press through the temptation and resist compromise. You will get your breakthrough!

## PRACTICAL APPLICATION

*Encouraging thoughts and scriptures to meditate on:*

- God is the Lord of the breakthrough! He is bringing me to victory. Second Samuel 5:20 says, "And David came to Baal-perazim, and he smote them there, and said, The Lord has broken through my enemies before me, like the bursting out of great waters. So he called the name of that place Baal-perazim [Lord of breaking through]."

- The calling and anointing upon my life are great. I may have opposition, but with God's help I will press through the persecution, criticism, and discouragement. Philippians 3:13–14 says, "I press on to take hold of that which Christ Jesus took hold of me."

    Nehemiah 4:14: "Don't be afraid of them. Remember the Lord, who is great and awesome."

- What God has placed in my heart to believe for, to build, and to dream are worth fighting for and I will not compromise those things. Nehemiah 4:14 says, "Fight for your families, your sons and your daughters, your wives and your homes."

    Ephesians 3:20: "Now to Him who is able to do exceedingly abundantly above all that we ask or think, according to the power that works in us."

### *Practical steps you can take:*

- I will not focus my eyes on the rubble of my life and what the enemy has sent to distract me. Instead, I will remember my Lord, who is great and awesome.

- I will strive to fully obey God and his Word and to live a no-compromise life that pleases him.

- I will press through until I see my breakthrough!

# 6

# Keep Calm and Shake It Off

❦

*Cast your burden on the Lord [release it] and He will sustain and uphold you.*

—Psalm 55:22

Not too long ago, I read Joyce Meyers's book *Overload*, and it was so good. In it she talks about practicing what she calls shrug therapy. I know it sounds funny, but it made sense to me. She said that there are some things in life we can control, like the friends we choose, the house we live in, or the car we drive. Then there are other things we cannot control, like the traffic and what people say or do. With the latter, we have a choice to make. We can allow those things to upset us and live a very stressful life, or we can simply shrug them off. We can store up stress and frustration or let God handle it. We can store up hurt, or we can release it to God. We can store up worry and fear, or we can shake them off!

To clarify, that doesn't mean you are nonchalant and don't care about anything. What it does mean is that, for the things you can't do anything about right now, you are not going to obsess over them. You are going to shrug them off and trust God to work them out for your good.

What does this look like for me? When I'm tempted to worry about things I cannot change, like where I am in the process of waiting for breakthrough, I must choose to shake it off and remember that God is in control. When you shake things off, it's a release! You are releasing that situation to God in faith.

Stress happens, and trials come to all of us, and too many times we hold on to the negative things. This is when you must choose not to take the burden on yourself. Psalm 55:22 says, "Cast your burden on the Lord [release it] and He will sustain and uphold you; He will never allow the righteous to be shaken (slip, fall, fail)" (AMP).

Your attitude and response to negative circumstances can cause you to be more stressed than the circumstances themselves. God wants you free from unnecessary baggage. Sin or a compromised lifestyle can lead to baggage, but there are other things that we should not stay attached to or carry as we await the fulfillment of God's promises. We're going to talk about those in this chapter, and we're going to talk about how to shrug or shake them off.

One of my favorite illustrations of this is found in Acts 28, where Paul found himself a castaway on an island called Malta. He and the crew had just been shipwrecked and the Maltans, being hospitable, kindled a fire for them. While he was adding more wood to the fire, Paul was bitten by a snake. The Bible says the snake fastened itself onto Paul's hand so tightly that Paul had to vigorously shake it off. After the frightening incident, Paul calmly went on about his business, not at all affected by the bite of this venomous snake. The people were dumbfounded: Was Paul a god? Not at all. But he knew who his God was and that this snake was not going to do any damage while Paul still had a purpose to live out. So you see how I got the title of this chapter now? Paul kept calm and shook it off.

The season of waiting for your breakthrough can be challenging and you may feel like you want to give in to all the negativity the enemy is sending your way. My word to you: don't do it. Learn from Paul and shake it off.

## Favor for the Storm

Before Paul ended up on Malta, he had been sentenced to serve time in prison in Rome for preaching about Jesus. Because he was arrested in Caesarea, a town in Israel, he had to be transported to Rome in order to serve his time there. While his enemies may have thought they were going to stop and silence him, God had a whole other plan in mind. God told Paul, "I have a purpose for you. I am sending you to Rome to share the gospel with Caesar." (See Acts 23:11.)

Paul was put on a ship for his journey to Rome, and the ship made several stops along the way. Just before the ship took off from one of the harbors, however, Paul—by the Holy Spirit—warned the captain not to set sail because the trip would end in disaster. But the captain didn't listen to Paul. After they'd set sail, all of a sudden they encountered a hurricane-force wind.

During this horrible storm, the prisoners, soldiers, and crew spent fourteen days without food and without seeing the sun. They thought they would perish, but Paul stood up and declared what God had spoken to him:

> I urge you to keep up your courage, because not one of you
> will be lost; only the ship will be destroyed. Last night an
> angel of the God to whom I belong and whom I serve stood
> beside me and said, "Do not be afraid, Paul. You must

> *stand trial before Caesar; and God has graciously given*
> *you the lives of all who sail with you." So keep up your*
> *courage, men, for I have faith in God that it will happen*
> *just as he told me. (Acts 27:22–26)*

This is what I believe God is saying to you today too. Even in the midst of the worst of trials, God has a purpose for you. He doesn't send the storms of life, but he will direct the storm for your sake. He will direct the winds in your favor. The other thing to remember is that sometimes people around you make decisions that affect your life in a negative way. Look at how the captain of the ship decided to ignore Paul's warning. As a prisoner, Paul had no choice but to go with them. His life was in danger because of someone else's decision.

Sometimes people do things that hurt you and that seem to affect your life and destiny, but you have to remember that this is not the end of the story. It may look like they have the upper hand, but God will turn it around for your good. So just as Paul stood among the passengers of that ship and spoke God's words over their situation, I release God's words over you today: Don't be depressed, because you will not perish! You will make it through the storm. Don't be afraid because you have a destiny to fulfill. Keep up your courage because God will protect you. You have favor for the storm you are going through right now! God will give you favor with the right people. As you trust God, favor is going to come on you in an increased measure!

And listen to this! Because of Paul—one godly man on that ship—God spared the lives of all the people on board. Paul was on a mission from God. He had to get to Rome. This was his destiny, and God wasn't going to allow anyone or anything to stand in his way!

It's amazing what God will do for one man or woman of faith. Don't worry about the people who are trying to hurt you or stop you. God will move heaven and earth just for you!

One of our worship leaders at Lakewood is Ramiro Garcia. He was not supposed to be able to hear or talk because of a birth defect. His parents were saddened and didn't know what to do, but he had a praying grandmother. She was a woman with great faith.

Everything changed when his grandmother stepped up and said, "God can heal Ramiro, and he is not only going to heal him, God is going to use him greatly!" And God did heal him completely, just as she believed. He is an amazing worship leader today.

One woman changed the course of Ramiro's life because she prayed a big prayer. She also changed the course of his family's life and now God has given Ramiro a platform to share Jesus with thousands of people. There is so much God wants to do through you, and he has given you favor for the storm you are in right now.

So we're back to where I began Paul's story at the beginning of the chapter: the passengers shipwrecked on Malta. The ship ran aground a distance from the beach, and the crew and the other passengers swam to shore on broken pieces of the ship. They made it by the skin of their teeth!

> The islanders showed us unusual kindness. They built a fire and welcomed us all because it was raining and cold. Paul gathered a pile of brushwood and, as he put it on the fire, a viper, driven out by the heat, fastened itself on his hand.
>
> When the islanders saw the snake hanging from his hand, they said to each other, "This man must be a murderer; for though he escaped from the sea, the goddess Justice has not allowed him to live."

> *But Paul* shook the snake off *into the fire and suffered*
> no ill effects. *The people expected him to swell up or sud-*
> *denly fall dead; but after waiting a long time and seeing*
> *nothing unusual happen to him, they changed their minds*
> *and said he was a god.* (Acts 28:1–6, NLT, emphasis added)

Because of this strange occurrence, the people were curious about what Paul believed, and he ended up sharing the gospel with everyone on that island. He then laid his hand on the sick, and every person was healed!

## Shake It Off!

You may be feeling like you are making it by the skin of your teeth. You may be saying, "There better not be one more bad thing happen to me or I don't know what I'll do." Can you imagine being Paul? After swimming to shore and finally getting on dry land, being warmed by a fire—it may have seemed like everything was finally going to be okay. They made it to shore. They didn't die. But then he got bitten by a snake.

I mean, really! What else could happen to this great man of God? It was like it was one bad thing after another, much like it can be for us. We get knocked down by the challenges in life, then we get back up. We get knocked down again, and we get back up only to be knocked down again and again. This is why I believe God put Proverbs 24:16 in the Bible. It says, "Though the righteous fall seven times, they rise again, but the wicked stumble when calamity strikes."

There's a difference between the righteous and the wicked,

between those who serve God and those who don't. We can get back up in times of disaster. We don't have to collapse because God is on our side.

Paul was imprisoned for preaching the gospel. He was on a ship that shipwrecked. And he had just been bitten by a poisonous snake. It was a series of unfortunate events. But Paul didn't bow to his circumstances. When that snake tried to attach itself to him, he didn't panic, though it could have killed him. He simply shook it off!

When he shook it off, all of a sudden things shifted in his favor. The people of Malta originally thought Paul was a murderer. After all, he was aboard a ship full of prisoners and guards. But after seeing how he shook off that snake and how there were no ill effects, they realized there was something different about him. They realized God had spared his life. Then every sick person on that island was healed when Paul prayed for them.

Malta was an island full of people who needed God. Paul may have been shipwrecked, but it was God who directed that storm so Paul could bring them salvation and healing. They had been worshipping idols, but through Paul they had an encounter with the living God. Paul may have thought he needed Malta during that storm, but the truth is Malta needed Paul, and God made sure he landed there. We must hold tightly to the promises of God and our dreams but hold loosely to how God is going to bring them to pass.

What was meant to kill Paul actually elevated him! The very thing you are facing today may have come to kill you, but God will cause it to elevate you! The things that happened to you as a child were meant to destroy your future, but God has a great future for you. The words people have spoken over you were meant to push you down and keep you from your destiny, but God is about to

> *What comes to kill you, God will cause it to elevate you.*

raise you up and give you a platform you could have never had on your own. But you know what you're going to have to get good at? Shaking it off.

There are some things in life you have to let go of. Some things will try to attach themselves to you, but, if you learn how to turn them loose, they never will. When you walk in your authority in the name of Jesus, things will shift. You actually change the atmosphere for miracles, healings, and salvations to take place. What was meant to destroy you will catapult you into your destiny.

## Have Faith in God

We can be going through trouble, but we don't have to remain in a state of stress and distress. Will we understand everything we go through? No, we won't but we can trust God for the things we can't control. Naturally, we are fixers. We want to know what the problem is. We want to be in control, and we want to change things. But for the things we can't change, Jesus said to "have faith in God" (Mark 11:22). Have faith in his Word. Numbers 23:19 says, "God is not human, that he should lie, not a human being, that he should change his mind. Does he speak and then not act? Does he promise and not fulfill?" Never. God always comes through. The writer of Psalm 37:25 says, "I was young and now I am old, yet I have never seen the righteous forsaken or their children begging bread." God never forsakes the righteous.

So if you're in control, you're going to have problems. But if God is in control, you're going to have victory. If God controls the situation, then we can control our response, which includes our attitude, our words and what we talk about, and on what we meditate. This is how we shake things off.

Jesus said, "Let not your heart be troubled; you believe God, believe also in Me" (John 14:1). The Amplified Bible says, "Let not your heart be troubled or distressed or agitated."

"Let not" means you have the choice. You can choose to shake it off or you can try to control everything. Remember God has given you a spirit of power, not a spirit of fear! Don't allow people or circumstances to steal your peace. You have the power of the Holy Spirit inside of you to help you walk in his peace as you trust God with your life.

When you start to feel a rush of distress, stop and say, "I'm not going down this road. I have a choice. I choose to trust God in this chaos. I am going to take hold of God's peace right now."

## Assume the Best

As you begin to trust God at new levels, learn not to assume the worst in a situation. Train yourself to assume the best. It may be part of our human nature to assume the worst, but I encourage you to shake off doubt and fear and say, "God, I believe You will cause everything to turn out for my good." Speak peace and confidence to your heart and mind by saying, "I expect everything to be okay. I expect a great future because that's what God's Word says. I expect victory. I expect the goodness of God in my life. I expect God's favor in this situation." David said in Psalm 27:13, "What would have happened to me if I would not have believed I would see the goodness of the Lord?" Believe that God has goodness stored up for you.

God said in Isaiah 52:12, "I will go before you and I will also be your rear guard." God's got you covered on all sides! Only he can be in front of you and behind you at the same time!

The Bible teaches us that we must learn to encourage ourselves. We discussed this earlier in chapter 3. It is something all believers need to learn to do. You cannot afford to wait until it's so bad that you can hardly get out of bed. Get ahead of discouragement, and start to recognize the downward spiral and catch it before it gets out of hand. When you feel it starting to close in, stop and say to yourself, "I'm shaking off this discouragement, and I'm going to encourage myself today." The deliberate and intentional action you take here will shift the atmosphere around you. Your faith will be built up, and you will be encouraged!

Another thing you can do to encourage yourself is to turn your worry into a prayer. This has changed my life! When I start to worry about anything, I stop and pray about it and thank God for taking care of the situation instead.

## A Magnet for Blessings

One of the messages of Paul's story is that you can't allow anything negative to attach itself to you; you can't allow any thoughts or beliefs to run unchecked in your mind and spirit. Understand that you are a magnet for blessings and favor, not for negative things. When negative thoughts come, shake them off. Stop accepting everything that comes your way. Shake off discouragement, hopelessness, lies from the enemy, insecurity, fear, and worry. These are some things you have to be very aggressive with.

The Bible says that we cannot be passive when it comes to the enemy. We are to "resist him, steadfast" (1 Pet. 5:9). As a child of God, you are not destined for disaster, despite what the enemy may be telling you. Resist his lies at every turn and receive God's thoughts toward you, which are good and not evil, to give you a future and a hope. You have to vigilantly reject what the enemy means for your harm and set yourself as a magnet for the blessing of God.

"Casting off" is another way the Bible helps us understand what it means to shake off the things that are not God's will for us. Let's look at this verse in the Amplified Version of the Bible:

> *Casting the whole of your care [all your anxieties, all your worries, all your concerns, once and for all] on Him, for He cares for you affectionately and cares about you watchfully. Be well balanced (temperate, sober of mind), be vigilant and cautious at all times; for that enemy of yours, the devil, roams around like a lion roaring [in fierce hunger], seeking someone to seize upon and devour. Withstand him; be firm in faith [against his onset—rooted, established, strong, immovable, and determined].*

Did you notice that, in addition to being instructed to cast your care on the Lord, this verse also exposes Satan as wanting to seize upon you quickly? He wants to catch you off guard and take hold of you suddenly and forcibly. This is why you must be vigilant about shaking things off as they come. Thoughts can come so quickly that they seem to knock you back for a moment, but you don't have to let them control you.

Say this aloud with me now: "Satan, I will not allow you to attach yourself to me. I resist you in the name of Jesus! Father, I am a magnet for your blessings, healing, provision, and protection."

Instead of giving in to worry and despair, give in to hope and peace and trust. Earlier, we looked at David's example. He was at the lowest point in his life, when he chose to take his thoughts captive and encourage himself in the Lord. The enemy had come into his city and taken all the women and children. David and his men wept until they could weep no more. Then they started playing

> *Instead of giving in to worry and despair, give in to hope and peace and trust.*

the blame game, wanting to pin it all on David. Instead of allowing despair, rejection, and hopelessness to run the show, David turned to God and encouraged himself.

What David was doing was shaking it off. I can imagine him saying something like this: "God, this may be the worst disaster of my life, but you are still my God. This story is not over yet! I trust you for the full turnaround and recovery of everything my enemies have taken. I reject the enemy's plan for my life and receive yours."

The Bible says that David rose up, went after the enemy, and recaptured every woman and child and the spoils that had been taken. David recovered all! He did not allow his emotions to control him, though he felt them. He did not allow a victim mentality to set in, because he knew God was on his side. He chose to believe God's best in the darkest time of his life—and shook off everything else that did not come into alignment with what he knew.

## Let Go and Let God

God is bringing restitution and restoration to your situation. He is going to bring vindication, and things are going to shift in your life as you shake off the things that come to weigh you down. Things are going to shift when you begin to walk in the authority that Jesus gave you over Satan. You don't have to sit and listen to his lies. You can keep calm because the peace of God that passes all understanding rules your heart (Col. 3:15). You can shake it off because you have power in the name of Jesus.

Perhaps you have been so burdened. You've been up against so many negative things. God is saying to you, "You don't have to carry all those burdens. Release them to me." Just as God desires to fight your battles for you, he also desires to carry your burdens for you. I want to say this to you again: keep your eyes on Jesus. Magnify God and not your circumstances.

If you know you have found yourself dwelling on the problem, God is saying, "It's time to shift your focus from the circumstances to me." It's time to let go of trying to do everything on your own. It's time to stop trying to be the fixer of every person and problem around you. Shake those things loose. Let them go and let God have his way. Trust God to be in control of all that concerns you.

He wants you to be free to walk in the fullness of joy. He wants to lift you up and bring you out of that pit of despair and hopelessness. You know, sometimes you have to just laugh in the face of hardship.

When one of our twin girls was around the age of ten, I walked into her bedroom to say goodnight. She was sitting on the bed and looked very frustrated. I asked her, "What's wrong, sweetie?"

She said, "Mom, I am so frustrated I don't know whether to cry, scream, or laugh."

I said, "Well, why don't we do all three together?"

That did it! She burst out laughing, but the night was not over until we both let out a loud scream! The laughter and joy we experienced that night encouraged both of us.

The Bible says, "The joy of the Lord is your strength" (Neh. 8:10), and in Job 5:22, it says, "You shall laugh at destruction and famine, and you shall not be afraid" (NKJV).

When things look bad around you, maybe it's time to experience the joy of the Lord. Habakkuk 3:17–18 says, "Though the fig tree does not bud and there are no grapes on the vines...yet I will rejoice in the LORD, I will be joyful in God my Savior." God wants to restore your laughter. He wants you to get your joy back.

In an act of faith, begin to let go. Cast your burdens on the Lord and allow him to restore your joy. As uphill as things may be, as dark and seemingly hopeless, you can choose to believe in God's good plan for your life. You can shake off the lies that come to tell you otherwise. You have favor to endure the storm you are in. Victory is in your DNA. Take hold of God and his Word! Take hold of God's peace. With God, you win, no matter what it looks like in your circumstances.

So with this truth holding you firm, you can keep calm and shake it off. You can even dance and laugh it off. Your sure victory is on the way.

Would you pray this prayer with me now? Let's cast your cares on the Lord and ask him to restore your joy again!

*Father, in the name of Jesus, I thank you for lifting oppression off of me. I command all despair and hopelessness to leave me now in the powerful name of Jesus.*

*Father, I pray that you will fill me with your joy and your peace that passes all understanding. I thank you, in advance, that I will laugh again. I will be joyful because of my decision to obey you. You are shifting things in my favor. I rejoice in you no matter what I am going through.*

*Thank you, Father, for rearranging things on my behalf. God, I see you moving people out of my life that need to be moved. I see you surrounding me with the right people.*

*I declare, in the name of Jesus, that this is a new day and a new season. The old is leaving and the new is coming. The fresh wind of your Spirit is blowing upon me like it never has before. Father, I thank you for your breath of life. Thank you for your breath of healing, your breath of joy, and your breath of promotion.*

*Thank you, Father, for all you are restoring to my life. In Jesus' name, amen.*

## PRACTICAL APPLICATION

### *Encouraging thoughts and scriptures to meditate on:*

- God promised to carry my burdens and sustain me in every situation. Psalm 55:22 says, "Cast your burden on the Lord [release it] and He will sustain and uphold you; He will never allow the righteous to be shaken (slip, fall, fail)" (AMP).

  John 14:4: "Let not your heart be troubled; you believe God, believe also in Me."

- God is giving me the favor I need today. Psalm 5:12 says, "Lord, you bless the righteous; you surround them with your favor as with a shield."

- God will cause everything to turn out for my good. Romans 8:28 says, "And we know that in all things God works for the good of those who love him."

Psalm 27:13: "I remain confident of this: I will see the goodness of the LORD in the land of the living."

### *Practical steps you can take:*

- I will not take hold of the negative things. I will keep calm and shake them off!

- I will turn my worries into prayers, thanking God that victory is on the way.

- I will assume and expect the best in my life. I expect a great future. I expect the goodness of God in my life.

# 7

# Don't Panic—This Is Just a Test

❧

*Their hearts are steadfast, trusting in the Lord. Their hearts are secure, they will have no fear.*

—Psalm 112:7–8

Years ago, Kevin and I went snowmobiling in Colorado with friends. We were on a guided tour, and I loved it! It was a beautiful view of the aspen trees and the snow. It was so much fun, until we got to this very steep hill. As I watched the snowmobiles in front of me go down the hill, I couldn't see the ground below them because it was so steep. It was like they were driving off into oblivion!

"Where's the ground? Where are these people going?" I started to panic.

I looked at Kevin, both of us hidden in all this snow gear, and shook my head, signaling to him, *No way. I'm not going down there.*

He used his hands, like an air traffic controller, motioning to me to *Go! Lisa, you can do it!*

But I didn't listen. Instead I threw on the brakes, but the ground was so slippery that my snowmobile started sliding sideways toward the hill. I knew I was going down that hill whether I liked it or not. That's when I really panicked, and the adrenaline kicked in. With not one ounce of athleticism in my body, I stood up on the snowmobile and dove off of it into the snow, leaving the unmanned snowmobile fishtailing down the hill all by itself!

I kept thinking, *Please don't crash. I don't want to pay for that snowmobile!* Fortunately, there was no damage to the snowmobile, only to my pride. I was so embarrassed! Not only that, but my reaction caused my friend to panic and she wouldn't go down the hill either. Kevin ended up taking me down the hill on his snowmobile. And you know what? We were just fine. I panicked for no reason. What's worse, I caused others to panic.

Panic can be contagious, but so can peace.

Often in life we are hit suddenly by difficulties, tragedy, financial problems, or sickness. Sometimes it's the long-term challenges that strike a blow. What do we do? One thing we don't want to do is to be overcome by panic.

*Panic* means "sudden uncontrollable fear or anxiety, often causing wildly unthinking behavior."[4] It can come over you in a split second. All of a sudden, we feel fear and chaos. But just because it happens doesn't mean we have to remain in that state of fear and panic. Second Timothy 1:7 says, "God did not give you a spirit of fear, but a spirit of power, love, and a sound mind." It's the spirit of power I want to emphasize.

As a believer, God has given you a spirit of power. That means you have the power of the Holy Spirit inside of you to do the right thing when panic and fear try to overtake you. You have power to resist panic and to remain in peace and with a sound mind.

When I panicked, I didn't have a sound mind. I didn't make

---

[4] Dictionary.com, s.v. "panic," https://www.dictionary.com/browse/panic?s=t.

good decisions. I made all the wrong choices. I'm so thankful I didn't get injured or have to pay for a damaged snowmobile.

God doesn't want you to remain in a state of panic. He wants you to walk in his peace. Take hold of his peace, the Bible says. We will face challenges and our first response may be panic, but we can move from overwhelming fear to overwhelming faith. God's Word is key to our being able to make this shift. Psalm 112 is a passage in Scripture that I read often to help me in this area. Let's look at this powerful passage now. I recommend you mark it as one of your go-to resources when panic tries to set up residence in your life. It says:

> *Praise the Lord. Blessed are those who fear the Lord, who find great delight in His commands. Their children will be mighty in the land; the generation of the upright will be blessed. Wealth and riches are in their houses, and their righteousness endures forever.*
>
> *Even in the darkness light dawns for the upright, for those who are gracious and compassionate and righteous. Good will come to those who are generous and lend freely, who conduct their affairs with justice.*
>
> *Surely the righteous will never be shaken; they will be remembered forever. They will have no fear of bad news; their hearts are steadfast, trusting in the Lord. Their hearts are secure, they will have no fear; in the end they will look in triumph on their foes. (emphasis added)*

Making it more personal, God is saying, "When you trust in me, I will be the light in your darkness. You will never be shaken. You will have no fear of bad news. Your heart will be secure. You will look in triumph on your enemies." In other words, don't panic; what you are facing is a test—a trust test. Are we going to trust God or fall apart? The Bible calls it the trial of our faith when we have to put the Word of God into practice.

Over the years as I have faced great challenges, I have learned that there are certain things I can do that help me remain in peace and faith, despite the panic I may be feeling. Let me share them with you.

## You Are in Control of Your Response

One of the first things you need to know is that you are always in control of your response. Philippians 4:6–7 tells us, "Do not be anxious about anything, but in every situation, by prayer and petition, with thanksgiving, present your requests to God. And the peace of God, which transcends all understanding, will guard your hearts and your minds in Christ Jesus."

> *We may feel afraid or feel panic, but we can choose peace. We can choose to trust God.*

In that moment when you experience panic and fear, ask God to fill you with his peace. It is a supernatural peace and calm that only he can give.

There are pivotal turning points in our lives when we must choose to trust God instead of allowing ourselves to be overtaken by panic and fear. Trusting God is not a feeling but a choice we make. We may feel afraid or feel panic, but we can choose peace. We can choose to trust God and tap into his peace that will guard our hearts and minds. This leads me to my next point.

## Listen to Your Spirit and Not Your Head

When panic comes, there's always an array of emotions and negative thoughts. That's normal. You can very easily make decisions based on how you feel, but if you ride the roller coaster of your emotions, you will be up, down, and all over the place. This is the time to tune in to your spirit more than ever because the Holy Spirit lives in you and he will help you and speak to you. The Word of God that you have read and meditated on will come up out of your spirit and speak to you as well. Actually, one of the first questions you should ask yourself is, "What does God's Word say?"

Imagine you had three volume controls on your body. When a sudden tragedy or setback happens, you would turn down the volume on your negative thoughts. You would turn down the volume on your emotions. But you would turn up the volume on your spirit. Don't allow negative thoughts and your emotions to drown out God's voice. Allow the Word of God to come up out of you and talk to you and encourage you. Let the Holy Spirit comfort you and lead you. Allow God's voice to be the dominant voice in your life.

> *Allow God's voice to be the dominant voice in your life.*

Years ago, I had the opportunity to put this advice to the test. I had been feeling sick for some time and was not able to get well. It was like I had some kind of weakness and infection in my body. I went to the doctor and later he called me with the results of the bloodwork. He began to explain to me that I had chronic fatigue syndrome and that it might take months to recover.

As he talked, I could feel the fear and panic rising up in me, but when I hung up the phone, I made a decision. I said to myself, "I'm not going to panic over this. In fact, I'm not going to have chronic fatigue syndrome. I'm going walk in healing."

In that second, I chose faith over fear and healing over sickness. I began to pray and declare the Word of God over my health, because that's what was in my spirit. Within a couple of weeks, I was strong and completely healed.


## Stop Overthinking

It is our natural bent to want to know how, why, when, and where. I am guilty of this too, so I know that we can waste so much time and energy trying to figure out things only God knows. We can become obsessed over things we can't understand or figure out. We have to realize there are times when we have to trust God with the unknown.

Jesus said, "Why take you thought saying, What shall we eat? What shall we drink? What shall we wear?" (Matt. 6:31). This truly shows how acquainted he is with our griefs and hardships. He understands how easy it is for us to start asking question after question: "What am I going to do? What is God going to do? How am I going to get out of this? What if this…? What if that…?" Jesus is also challenging us with "Why do you do that, working yourself into a panic?"

We think we have to know and we need to know everything, but that is not true. God will reveal to us the things we need to know. And if he chooses not to—we can be at peace with that. You can simplify your life by simplifying your thoughts. Let go of all the questions and trust God with the answers. Again, it is a trust test.

> *You can simplify your life by simplifying your thoughts.*

I remember going through a very difficult time after I went through an unwanted divorce in my early twenties. I kept tormenting myself with all the unknown questions: "Why did this happen to me? What could I have done differently?" On and on, I asked the Lord question after question.

Finally God spoke to me so clearly and said, "Stop asking questions and realize that you have an enemy who is seeking to destroy you."

That day, I stopped asking questions about that situation, and I chose instead to acknowledge the real enemy. Satan is the enemy of our souls. He wanted me to remain in a state of depression and guilt. He wanted to keep me from my purpose.

When God made it clear to me that it was the enemy trying to wreak havoc in my life, it was a turning point for me. I stood in a whole new place of confidence and declared, "Satan will not triumph over me! I will not play his game! I will trust God with my life and move forward!" I can't tell you the freedom I've walked in since that day. God is so good!

Just like I learned at that stage of my life, you have the power to speak to the storm in your life. When Jesus was in the boat with his disciples and a storm arose, the disciples began to panic. Jesus simply stood up and spoke to the storm, "Peace, be still" (Mark 4:39). The Bible says next that there was a great calm. He used the power he had and in turn showed the disciples that they had power too. "I have given you authority to trample on snakes and scorpions and to overcome all the power of the enemy; nothing will harm you" (Luke 10:19).

I want to encourage you to pull from the faith deep in your spirit—everyone has at least a mustard seed—and speak to the storm in your mind and say, "Peace, be still!"

Psalm 46:10 says, "Be still and know that he is God"! Be still in your mind and allow God's peace to prevail. The Passion Translation says, "Surrender your anxiety! Be silent and stop your striving and you will see that I am God." You will witness a great calm and the power of God in your life!

## Pray About It

Shifting my worrisome thoughts to prayer has helped me so much. I mentioned this in an earlier chapter, but I say it again here, because this practice amped up my prayer life. I pray a lot more now. Philippians 4:6 says, "Don't worry about anything, but pray about everything." The apostle wrote these words as he was sitting in a small prison cell for preaching the gospel. Can you imagine what he was going through? He had so many reasons to be anxious, yet he chose not to worry. He chose prayer instead.

> *Turn every worried thought you have into prayer or thanksgiving.*

You can do this too. For example, if a fearful thought comes to your mind like this: "What if something bad happens to me?" Instead of entertaining the thoughts and mounting on more questions, pray a prayer something like this: "Father, I thank you that I have no fear of bad news. You are taking care of me and my family. Something good is going to happen to me. I know victory is on the way!"

Worry stirs up fear, but prayer stirs up the supernatural! Prayer takes you into another level of thinking and living, into a peace that only God can give. The Bible calls it a peace that passes all understanding.

> *Prayer takes you into another level of thinking and living, into a peace that only God can give.*

## Choose Love

Before we leave this chapter, there is another part to this test to choose trust over panic that I want us to look at and that is the people factor. In almost every crisis, we have to deal with people. The truth is, sometimes people are the crisis! They are the ones stirring up the trouble. Possibly someone cheated you out of money, betrayed you, or unjustly fired you from a job.

If we are not careful, we will panic and begin to think that people have power over our lives and our destiny. But they don't! So what is our response?

Jesus said, "Love your enemies and pray for those who persecute you" (Matt. 5:44). Instead of getting upset over what people are doing and saying, pray for them, love them, forgive them, and bless them. Then trust God to vindicate you.

Even as you pray for them and forgive them, it doesn't mean you have to hang around them. Sometimes we have to love people from a distance. But if we are not careful, we will allow them to pull us into their fight and act like they're acting. This is what you don't want. I love what my brother Joel says: "People are not in control of your life, God is. It may look like they are in control, but they are actually pawns in God's hand."

Ephesians teaches us that we wrestle not against flesh and blood. We don't fight like the world. We use our spiritual weapons to fight a spiritual battle. We love people when they hate. We pray for people when they mistreat us. We overcome evil with good. (See Romans 12:21.)

Remember, this is a test—a trust test. When you love God, you trust him enough to obey, even with hard matters like blessing those who do you wrong.

There is a man in our church who grew up without a father present in his life. His parents divorced when he was young, and he was very angry that his father abandoned them. As a teen, he rebelled and almost ended up in prison, but for the grace of God, he had a praying mother.

My friend will tell you that he had father issues and that it was affecting his life. This led him to pray. As he took the matter to God, his heart began to soften toward his father. Soon, he reached out to his father to see how they could begin to build their relationship where there was not much of a relationship at all.

One day, the Lord impressed upon this man to apologize to his father for holding anger in his heart toward him. He also repented to him because he felt he had dishonored his dad for so long by talking bad about him to other family members. Any time his name came up in a conversation he had something negative to say about his father. He had come to understand that if he wanted to be fully restored, he would have to lay down anger and take up love and forgiveness toward his father.

As the father and son were out to lunch, the son wept and apologized to his father. His father also began to weep and said, "No, I need to apologize to you."

That was the beginning of the process of healing.

The father hadn't been there for his children in many of the ways they may have needed while growing up, but one night the Lord spoke to the son to give his father some money. The father couldn't believe it and didn't want to accept it. It seemed like it should have been the other way around—the father should help the son. But, you see, this man was allowing God to direct him into healing and restoration.

My friend wanted to honor his father even though he had not been the best father in the past. Those two acts of obedience broke down walls that had stood for years. The father soon called his children together and apologized to each of them. They wept together, and he gave them each a financial gift.

Now there is restoration. This son has a relationship with his father. He is free and no longer controlled by hurt, anger, and rebellion. And the father is free to love his children again. That is what God can do when we choose to listen to the Holy Spirit and walk in love.

## A Prisoner of Hope

My friend's story of restoration helps us see what it is like to be set free from being prisoners to our emotions, circumstances, people, and negative thoughts. That is not where God wants us to set up residence. Instead we can be like the psalmist who made a choice to pitch his "tent in the land of hope" (Acts 2:26, THE MESSAGE). This is where we live, because there are no hopeless cases with God.

Zechariah 9:12 says that we are all prisoners of hope. God says, "Return to your fortress, O prisoners of hope; even now I announce that I will restore twice as much to you." We carry this identity because Jesus is our hope of glory. This hope is an anchor for our souls.

We can't even have faith without hope, as it is the substance of things hoped for. (See Hebrews 11:1.)

In I Kings 18, God spoke to Elijah and said, "I'm going to bring rain on the land," but at first, there was no sign of rain. Still, Elijah went up to the top of Mount Carmel and began to look for rain. He said to his servant, "Go look to see if there are any signs of rain."

His servant came back and said, "There is nothing."

But hope doesn't give up, so Elijah said to him, "Go back and look again." Five more times Elijah told the servant to go back and look. Each time, there still was no sign of rain.

By the seventh time, the servant came back and said, "I see a small cloud the size of a man's hand rising from the sea!"

Elijah said, "That's it! That's what I was hoping for and looking for!"

Then the sky grew black, and it began to rain! Elijah was a prisoner of hope!

A prisoner of hope stands firm in the position that says, "I'm looking for the rain." They expect God to take care of them. They expect the goodness of God in their life! A prisoner of hope knows God is on their side. They feel no need to panic because they know victory is on the way!

---

## PRACTICAL APPLICATION

*Encouraging thoughts and scriptures to meditate on:*

- God has given me a spirit of power to resist the urge to panic and remain in peace. Second Timothy 1:7 says, "God did not give you a spirit of fear, but a spirit of power, love, and a sound mind."

- I am in control of my response to difficulties and can choose to trust God and pray about everything. Philippians 4:6–7 says, "Do not be anxious about anything, but in every situation, by prayer and petition, with thanksgiving, present your requests to God. And the peace of God, which transcends all understanding, will guard your hearts and your minds in Christ Jesus."

- My heart is steadfast, trusting in the Lord and I will never be shaken. Psalm 112:6–8 says, "Surely the righteous will *never be shaken*; they will be remembered forever. They will have *no fear* of bad news; their hearts are *steadfast, trusting* in the Lord. Their hearts are *secure*, they will have *no fear*; in the end they will look in *triumph* on their foes."

### *Practical steps you can take:*

- I will choose peace over panic and prayer instead of worry.

- I will allow my spirit to be the most dominant voice in my life.

- I will not overthink my situation. Instead, I will always be a prisoner of hope.

# 8

# What Trusting God Looks Like

༄

*Trust in the Lord with* all *your heart.*

—Proverbs 3:5

In the last chapter, we saw how trusting God helps us view and handle our circumstances differently. When we trust God, we will see him as the light in our darkness. We will stand firm and never be shaken. We will not fear bad news. Our hearts will be secure and not panicked. We will look triumphantly on our enemies!

I want to go a little deeper into what trusting God really looks like. Sometimes we can hear about something, some bit of advice, and not really understand what it should look like lived out in our everyday lives.

Many times, we say, "I'm trusting God," but the truth is we are an emotional wreck. We are full of worry, fear, and doubt. I know because I have been there.

Several years ago, we were facing a difficult situation and one of my daughters asked me, "Mom, what are we going to do?"

I replied, "We're going to trust God to work this situation out."

My daughter said to me, "How can you just say that? How can you be so sure of that?"

I said to her, "Because I have walked with God a long time—and I have experienced his faithfulness and I know he will take care of us."

It's true! When you have walked with God—and have a personal relationship with him—you begin to understand his character and his faithfulness. You learn that you can trust his ways and his Word. You can trust his process, though it may be a different process than you desired. You can even trust his mysteries because sometimes we don't understand God.

Deuteronomy 29:29 tells us, "The secret things belong to the Lord our God." There are some things God doesn't reveal to us. With God, we are on a need-to-know basis. He knows what we can handle. But that scripture goes on to say that "God will reveal to us the things we need to know."

So when I said to my daughter that we were going to trust God, I didn't say it in a flippant or nonchalant way. My statement came with weight, depth, and confidence in knowing God is who he says he is—and he will do what he said he will do. He is I Am, the faithful and true God!

Today, you can know and confidently say, "I will trust God through this trial. When my child has gone astray. When I have financial needs. When I can't see him working because I know he is faithful!" There is a depth to those words that you must come to understand in your own life. You *can* trust God!

Proverbs 3:5–6 says, "Trust in the Lord with *all* your heart and lean not on your own understanding; in *all* your ways submit to him, and he will make your paths straight" (emphasis added). Notice the word *all* used twice. When you trust the Lord with *all* your heart and in *all* of your ways, he will make your paths straight. The Message translation says that "God will keep you on track."

I use this verse to pray over my family often: "Father, I thank you that because we trust you, you are making all of our ways straight. You are leading us on the right path."

I imagine that you are being forced to totally trust God right now, and it may be uncomfortable to you. You don't like not knowing and not being in control. Nobody does. We discussed how it totally goes against our nature. But the more you learn to relax and trust God, the more comfortable it becomes. You begin to settle into it. It becomes a way of life.

*Trust* is defined as "the assured reliance on the character, ability, strength, or truth of someone or something. One in which confidence is placed."[5] This is exactly what I am encouraging you to do: Simply trust God in the situation you are in right now. Trust his character and ability. Trust that he is in control. Trust that he has you covered.

To help you see what it means to trust God, I want to give you a picture or a plan of trust. I am going to use the word *trust* as an acronym to do it.

T = Test
R = Rest
U = Uproot
S = Stand
T = Timing

Let's now see what this looks like in action.

---

[5] Merriam-Webster.com, s.v. "trust," https://www.merriam-webster.com/dictionary/trust.

## *T* stands for "TEST"

Trust means you understand that the trial you're in is a test of your faith, and you must see it for what it really is. It's not from God, but your faith is being tested. We have already established this point, but I do want to remind you that God is not punishing you or ignoring you. Every person faces difficulty. This is a test—and James said, "If you persevere, you will become mature and lack nothing." (See James 1:2–4, 12.)

How can you trust God in the test? One way is to remain faithful to him. Since we know that God is faithful to us in every way, let's be faithful to him in every situation. God prizes a faithful person. Jesus taught us that a person who is faithful in the small things would be blessed with more. Second Chronicles 16:9 says, "For the eyes of the Lord run to and fro throughout the whole earth, to show Himself strong on behalf of those whose heart is loyal to Him." God longs to show himself strong on your behalf as you faithfully trust him.

God spoke to Abraham one time and asked him to leave his relatives and country in order to follow him. God had great plans for Abraham, but he shared no details or blueprint of what that would look like. It was like stepping out into the unknown. Abraham faithfully trusted God and followed him, without even knowing where he was going. God proved faithful to Abraham, who became the father of many nations and the father of our faith. (See Genesis 12:1–2.)

Like Abraham, we must faithfully trust God in the test though we do not see his whole plan. When we do not see how the situation could turn around. God's ways are not our ways, and yet he can be trusted.

Another way you can pass the test of your faith is by maintaining a thankful attitude. I often remember what the apostle Paul said in 1 Thessalonians 5:18: "Give thanks in all circumstances; for this is the will of God in Christ Jesus for you." I want to emphasize that we must be grateful *in* the circumstances, not necessarily *for* the circumstances. Sometimes we get focused on what's wrong with our lives, but we must remember all that is right in our lives. We have Jesus! We woke up today! There are many things we can be grateful for every day of our lives.

> *What does trust look like? It is being faithful to God during this test of your faith.*

## *R* stands for "REST"

The Prophet Isaiah reminds us that it is in quietness and trust that you will find strength. (See Isaiah 30:15.) When you put your total trust and dependence on God, you will be at rest. Trust and rest go hand in hand. Trust is not all tangled up in worry, fear, and frustration. It does not take you on an emotional roller coaster all the time. Trusting brings rest to your soul. So, if you are trusting, then you are resting. You are abiding in God's peace.

A few years ago, I told our kids that I wanted to bless them with a little money as a reward for being so supportive and patient with me when I was writing my first book. They were very excited. I told them that they could have the money whenever they needed it.

Our young son Christopher asked me several times, "Where's my money?"

I told him the same thing each time: "It's in the bank, but it belongs to you. Whenever you need it just let me know. You can trust me."

I understood the concept was a little hard for him to grasp as a child because he wanted to see the cold, hard cash in front of him. We can be this way sometimes. We may ask, "God, can you just give me a sign and then I will rest?"

Then God says to us, "It's in the bank! The answer is on the way! Rest in knowing that you can trust me."

Psalm 91:1 says, "He who dwells in the shelter of the Most High will REST in the shadow of the Almighty. I will say of the LORD, 'He is my refuge and my fortress, my God, in whom I trust.'"

I think sometimes we feel the need to help God out. We think, *How can I possibly rest when I have such problems? I have to do something about this. I have to fix this problem!*

The problem with that is that sometimes we end up being more frustrated and anxious.

Psalm 94:13 says that God gives you the power to keep yourself calm in the days of adversity, but are we allowing God's peace to rule and reign in our minds and emotions? If we aren't, we need to tap into the reservoir of supernatural peace available to us through Christ.

A few years ago, our daughter Catherine and I were driving to Dallas, where she was going to college. I heard a noise as if a car in front of us had run over something in the road. All of a sudden, I saw this piece of plywood—that was about four feet by four feet—flying in the air toward our windshield.

In a split second, I thought, *It's heading through the windshield straight to us.* But at the last second it hit the hood, angled upward, and flew right over the top of our car. It was over so quick. I knew God had literally protected us and caused that plywood to move out of our direction.

What's amazing is I had such a calm in me the whole time. My heart never raced, and I never became fearful. It was a supernatural rest and peace that settled upon me. I kept thanking God for not only protecting us but for giving me the power to remain calm in that situation. Only God can do that! It's supernatural!

Trust knows that even in the chaos, you can rest in the fact that God is still in control. I encourage you to let go of frustration and anger and doubt and fear and the stress of trying to work things out by yourself. Pray aloud right now: "God, help me to tap into your rest and peace and let go of frustration and worry."

> *What does trust look like? It is a picture of rest.*

## *U* stands for "UPROOT"

There are some things that we have to uproot in our lives in order to receive from God and walk in the rest I've been referring to. The first things we need to uproot are the lies of Satan.

Jesus said that Satan is a liar and the father of all lies. So it makes sense that he is going to bombard your mind with lies during this test. Jesus also said that Satan comes to steal, kill, and destroy. The number one way he does that is through your mind and your thoughts. Recognizing this truth is half the battle. (See John 8:44; 10:10.)

We must stay alert and guard our thoughts. We have to recognize when our thoughts don't agree with God's thoughts. When we hear thoughts like...

"Give up."
"I am not going to make it."
"I can't take one more day of this."
"God doesn't care about my life."

"I am a failure."

"I ruined my life."

... we need to know right away those are not our thoughts. They are thoughts the enemy is planting to get us to quit, to tap out, and to fail. But you cannot allow Satan's lies to stick, take root, or take up residence in your mind. My friend Debra says that some thoughts have been living in your mind so long they should be paying rent! It is time to evict those lies! They have to go!

Second Corinthians 10:5 tells us how to deal with these lies. It teaches us that lies can take a stronghold in our minds and lives if we dwell on them and believe them. It says that we are to pull down those strongholds and take those negative thoughts captive. We are to nip them in the bud when they come, and instead make our thoughts obedient to God's Word.

Then *you* control your thoughts instead of your thoughts controlling you. You make them obedient to God's Word. You replace the lies with God's powerful Word and truth! That's how you uproot the enemy's lies. You always combat lies with truth. By focusing your thoughts on God's thoughts, your emotions and life become more stable.

Practically, you call out the lie for what it is and replace it with a Scripture passage. There was a time in my life when I felt like I had missed my purpose and calling because of what I had been through. For a time, every night before I went to bed this thought would bombard my mind: *Another day and nothing has changed or improved in your life.*

> *What does trust look like? Uprooting negative thoughts and focusing on God's thoughts.*

I was so tempted to take the bait and go down that discouraging path, but I had to pull that thought down. I would immediately think, *That is a lie because I know the plans that God has for me are good and not evil, to give me a hope and a future!* Eventually, I didn't have that negative thought anymore because I refused what the enemy was speaking into my life.

## *S* is for "STAND"

Trust is a stand of faith and a position of power that we take as believers. This is what God said to Moses, "Don't be afraid. Stand firm and you will see My deliverance today. I will fight for you; you need only to be still" (Exod. 14:13–14).

To stand firm means you don't sit down in defeat! It means that you don't give up on God, his Word, your dreams, and your desires.

Ephesians 6:13–14 says, "Therefore put on God's complete armor, that you may be able to resist and stand your ground on the evil day [of danger], and having done all [the crisis demands], to stand [firmly in your place]. Stand therefore [hold your ground]" (AMP).

Based on this we learn that to stand means to hold your ground against Satan. Don't let him steal the promise from you. Hold your ground against the circumstances. Don't give up because of what is going on around you! Then you stand on God's Word and keep going. You stand and pray instead of worrying. You stand and praise God instead of talking about your problems. You stand and worship God instead of worshipping your circumstances. Stand and offer the sacrifice of thanksgiving instead of complaining about your life! Having done all the crisis demands, stand firmly in your place.

Stand in faith, knowing God is working on your behalf. Even in your greatest disappointments—when someone betrays you or walks out on you or when you lose your job—God is with you and he is working in your life.

Trust is standing with expectation, with a song of praise in your mouth, knowing that God will fight for you and deliver you.

My brother Joel tells the story about a time he went for a two-hour hike in the mountains of Colorado. He was over 10,000 feet high in altitude. Joel is very strong and athletic. He works out all the time. Still, altitude can affect even the fittest person.

At one point on the hike, he thought, *Man, I'm having shortness of breath. This is a little hard. I don't know if I'm going to make it all the way.* He sat down on this big rock to rest, and just as he was contemplating whether he should keep going or turn back, an older gentleman came walking by at a fast pace. He didn't even greet Joel. All he did was look at him and say, "You're closer than you think." With that recharge, Joel got up and finished the hike, discovering that he was indeed much closer to the top than he'd realized.

There are times in life when we get tired and we want to sit down. We feel like we can't make it to the next hour, let alone the next day. It seems that we have been waiting so long, but God is saying to us, "You're closer than you think. Don't give up before the victory."

> *What does trust look like? It's a picture of you standing firm in faith, knowing the victory is closer than you thought.*

## *T* stands for "TIMING"

The timing of your dream being fulfilled or your prayer being answered belongs to God—and as much as we would like to, we can't rush God! We discussed in chapter 1 that at the appointed time, God would bring the dream or the vision to pass. Psalm 31:15 says, "Our times are in His hands." I love how the Passion Translation reads: "My life, my every moment, my destiny—it's all in your hands. So I know you can deliver me from those who persecute me relentlessly."

Now, certainly we can cooperate with God, but I am talking about when you've done all you know to do; you have to trust God with the time.

This is the thing about not trusting God's timing. When we get impatient, we end up trying to help God out. We take matters into our own hands—and that's scary! Because we usually end up messing things up and causing delays.

Do you remember Abraham's wife Sarah? She did this. She got tired of waiting to have her own baby, even though God promised her she would have one. One day, she got fed up and decided she would take matters into her own hands. She asked Abraham to have a child with her servant Hagar.

It seems so easy for us to judge her or wonder what she was thinking. But we have our ways of trying to take matters into our own hands too! Sarah's plan was not God's plan, and it ended up bringing strife and heartache into her life, when all she had to do was wait on God.

Galatians 6:8 says that when we sow to the flesh, we reap of the flesh. But when we sow to the Spirit, we reap of the Spirit. It's when we wait on God's timing that we get the best harvest ever!

> *What does trust look like? You patiently waiting on God's timing.*

Look at the acronym for trust again. Let it imprint on your heart and mind:

T = Test

R = Rest

U = Uproot

S = Stand

T = Timing

Keep this list in mind, and realize that what you are going through right now is temporary. It's a test of your faith, but you can rest because you will pass the test if you are quick to uproot those lies. Stand firm in your faith, and trust God's timing.

## PRACTICAL APPLICATION

*Encouraging thoughts and scriptures to meditate on:*

- I can confidently trust God to help me through every challenge and adversity. Proverbs 3:5–6 says, "Trust in the Lord with *all* your heart and lean not on your own understanding; in *all* your ways submit to him, and he will make your paths straight."

- God longs to show himself strong on my behalf. Second Chronicles 16:9 says, "For the eyes of the Lord run to and fro throughout the whole earth, to show Himself strong on behalf of those whose heart is loyal to Him."

- I can trust God's timing for my life because he knows what is best for me. Psalm 31:15 says, "My life, my every moment, my destiny—it's all in your hands. So I know you can deliver me from those who persecute me relentlessly."

### *Practical steps you can take:*

- I will control my thoughts instead of allowing them to control me.

- I will let go of frustration, anger, doubt, and stress because I can trust God to give me his best.

- God is giving me the power to remain calm in any and all situations.

# 9

# God Is Planning a Resurrection

∾

*I am the resurrection and the life. The one who believes in me will live.*

—John 11:25

God loves to do the impossible for his children. I imagine you have come to this book facing something that seems impossible. Whether it's a relationship gone bad or a financial setback, God wants you to know that he delights in doing the impossible for you. I say this with such confidence because I've been where you are. I've gone through times in my life when I thought the situation was too far gone to be redeemed. But in one of these moments, God spoke a word to me that I've never forgotten. He said, "Lisa, I delight to do the impossible."

That was an on-time word for me. With the odds stacked against me, I needed to hear God say those words. It seemed impossible to me. I couldn't see a way out. That word touched my spirit and became revelation to me.

I realized that it didn't matter what I could not see or do myself.

What matters is that I serve a God who can do what I cannot do! He's a mighty and good God who wants to do the impossible for you too. Why? It's not complicated like we often make it. He does the impossible because he loves you!

Matthew 7:11 says, "If you then, being evil, know how to give good gifts to your children, how much more will your Father who is in heaven give good things to those who ask him!" The Bible also reminds us that nothing is impossible with God, and what is impossible with men is possible with God. God delights to give us the gift of his doing the impossible. He loves to do for us what we can't do for ourselves. He is a good and loving father.

After God spoke that word to me, I had gone on with my normal routine, minding my own business. My spirit had been lifted and I was feeling so much better. Then God spoke to me again and said, "Read John 11."

I love that you don't have to be on your knees to hear from God. When you spend time with God on a daily basis, you learn to hear his voice. He will speak to you anytime during the day. It's a voice or impression that you hear deep down in your spirit. And now that he seemed to be so near and speaking so clearly, I couldn't wait to get my Bible and see what John 11 said.

What I discovered was the story of Lazarus being raised from the dead. And as I read it, God showed me more about the impossible he desires to do in our lives. It encouraged me so much at a time when I really wasn't sure anything could be worked out. This is why the miracles were written and recorded in the Bible. They were written for you and for me to encourage us, to build our faith, to reveal God's will to us—and to show us that his supernatural power is available to us today (John 20:30–31).

Even as you are reading this book full of Bible verses, I encourage you to have your own Bible near. As you read John 11, you will notice from the start that there was a process to this miracle. Mary and Martha didn't get their answer the first day. They had sent a message to Jesus telling him that their brother was sick and might die: "Lord, the one you love is sick" (v. 3). But Jesus didn't come. In fact, the Bible says he stayed where he was two more days, before deciding to go to his friend Lazarus. By the time he arrived, it was already too late. Lazarus had died.

Of course we know the end of the story, but things got worse before they got better. Isn't that how it is sometimes? But even when things go from bad to worse, we must keep trusting, obeying, and expecting God to do the impossible.

We know that when Jesus arrived in Bethany, the town where his friends lived, Lazarus had been buried for four days. There was much sadness and grief. Everyone was weeping. Martha approached Jesus and said, "'Lord, if you had been here, my brother would not have died. But I know that even now God will give you whatever you ask'" (vv. 21–22).

Jesus let her know, without a flinching doubt, "Your brother will rise again." Martha reminded Jesus that after four days in the grave, Lazarus's body would stink. Jesus, the resurrection and the life, wasn't moved by that and called Lazarus from beyond the grave and raised him back to life.

Let me tell you now: If something is dead in your life, don't put on your grave clothes yet! This story proves to us that God specializes in raising dead things back to life. Whatever seems dead that you had been praying for, don't bury it yet. If God has put a dream in your heart, don't give up on seeing it come to pass. Wait on God and let him resurrect it!

It may be so dead that it stinks, but I want to tell you that it is never too late for a miracle! Just ask Lazarus! God can resurrect your health, your joy, your finances, your marriage, and your dreams! He has done it so many times for me!

If you have a child away from God, he can resurrect their life and potential and set them on a new path! If you have gone through heartache and disappointment, God can resurrect your purpose and the destiny he has called you to. God specializes in resurrecting dead things.

Let me give you more truths about this story that will help you.

## A Miracle Always Begins with a Need or a Problem

If you are in trouble or you have a problem, you qualify for a miracle. We all want to be overcomers, but we don't like the idea of having to face anything that needs overcoming. The raising of Lazarus is a great miracle, but don't forget that it began with a great problem. Mary and Martha were heartbroken because their brother died an early death. It looked hopeless.

Sometimes we complain about having to go through trials, but it's in the trials that we see the power of God manifested. So if you have a need or problem, look at it this way: You are a candidate for a miracle. This is an opportunity for God to show himself strong on your behalf.

As you face your problem, you must seek the Lord and his wisdom in your time of need. That's the first thing Mary and Martha did. They immediately sent for Jesus. This is the first thing you must do as well. He is the one who is going to sustain and carry you through the trials of life.

Some people respond to their problems by getting mad at God. They blame God for their problems. Some people respond to their problems by getting bitter: "Why did this have to happen to me?" Many people think that the problems of life are what ruin their lives, but they are not. It's how you respond to the problems that makes the difference.

Mary and Martha could have said, "Jesus, Lazarus is your friend! Why did you let this happen to him?" But they realized that Jesus was the one who could help them. They simply said, "Jesus, the one *you* love is sick." That touched the heart of Jesus. That's all he needed to hear.

When we are in trouble, we need to call on the name that is above every name—Jesus! He said, "Call upon Me and I will answer you and show you great and mighty things that you do not know" (Jer. 33:3). He said, "If you need wisdom, ask Me and I will give it to you liberally" (James 1:5).

Psalm 91 teaches us that when you call on him, he will rescue you, protect you, answer you, be with you in trouble, deliver you, honor you, satisfy you with long life, and show you his salvation and deliverance. These are promises we can hold on to!

One time I was talking to the Lord about some things going on in my life. I said, "Lord, I don't know the answers to some of these things."

Responding, the Lord spoke to my spirit and said, "You don't have to know all the answers as long as you know me."

You may not understand everything right now—but call out to the one who does!

## Hold on to the Promises of God

When Jesus first heard that Lazarus was sick, he sent word back to Mary and Martha and said, "Tell them that this sickness will not end in death." That was their promise from Jesus. Don't you know that they were excited and hung on that promise? They could actually say, "Jesus told me that everything is going to be all right!"

What you have to realize is that the Bible is God speaking to you. It is full of his promises for you and your family. But you have

> *If you will carry the Word in your heart, the Word will carry you through the trials of life.*

to search it out for yourself. You have to read the Word and meditate on it until it gets down into your spirit and becomes alive and powerful in you and produces faith in your heart!

If you will carry the Word in your heart, the Word will carry you through the trials of life. God told Joshua that if he wanted to be prosperous and successful, then he would have to put the Word in his heart and in his mouth. He would have to meditate on it day and night and be careful to obey everything written in it (Josh. 1:8).

You say, "Well, that's hard work. I didn't know I was going to have to work so hard for a miracle. I'm too busy watching TV. I have to get on social media. I just want someone to pray over me so I will get my miracle."

Miracles don't just happen. You have to set things in motion with your faith, like Mary and Martha did.

## God Doesn't Work on Your Timetable

You have to understand that usually there is waiting involved in seeing your prayers answered. This is when you have to exercise your faith and your patience. If you don't have any patience, this is where you get to develop it, because God doesn't work on our timetable. The quicker you get that in your head, the better off you will be. God carries out his will in his perfect timing and precision.

When Mary and Martha sent for Jesus, he didn't jump on a donkey or camel and rush to see Lazarus. In fact, Lazarus died before he got there. I'm sure that was hard for Mary and Martha. It looked like Jesus didn't care, like God wasn't listening.

I can imagine Mary saying, "Hold on, Lazarus, Jesus will be here." But for two days, there was nothing. They needed God now, but he wasn't showing up. To those looking on, it may have seemed like things were coming unraveled quickly. Jesus knew exactly what he was doing, and Mary and Martha held on to their faith.

Just because it hasn't happened yet doesn't mean it isn't going to happen. As I mentioned earlier, miracles are not always instant. Yet, we must hold on to the fact that just because we don't see God working, doesn't mean he isn't.

When Jesus finally showed up, Martha said, "Lord, if You had been here, my brother would not have died. But even now I know that whatever You ask of God, God will give You" (John 11:21–22). That's faith talking. That's someone who trusts God's timing.

I call this Martha kind of faith, "even-now faith." It's the kind of faith that says, "God, I know Lazarus has been dead four days, but even now I know that you can resurrect him!" "God, my son is away from you, but *even now* I believe you are working in his life!" Even-now faith says, "God, I have this disease in my body, but *even now* I know you can heal me!" Do you have "even now" faith? The kind of faith that doesn't give up when something looks dead in your life? The kind of faith that says, "God, I don't care how bad the situation is—even now I know you will do the impossible"?

My friends Irene and Polo have that even-now faith. Polo had a business partner who took advantage of him. His partner got him into all kinds of debt and financial trouble, and they ended up owing so much money to the IRS that it would devastate them financially. In the middle of all this, Polo had to have back surgery.

The IRS was calling them constantly, and the first time they met with their appointed agent they explained the situation and how they had never missed paying their taxes. They requested to pay the amount monthly since they didn't have enough money. The agent was rude and demanded the full amount immediately. Things just seemed to get worse.

But my friends knew how to pray. Irene prayed specifically, "God, you're going to have to send an angel to help us. We always honor you with our money and you said you would rebuke the devourer for our sake (Mal. 3:10–12). And I pray that you will move that agent off of our case." Now, that's a bold prayer!

They received a phone call to meet with a new agent. Irene asked, "What about our original agent?"

The answer was, "They transferred her to another state!"

When you pray bold prayers, you get bold answers. They met with their new agent, who was the sweetest lady. Irene said there was just something different about her. They told her what had happened and said, "We don't have all the money now, but we will pay you in increments if you allow us to."

The woman, or the angel—whomever she was—said, "Why don't you write out a check for one hundred dollars, and this will all be settled."

Out of amazement and appreciation Irene said, "A hundred dollars!"

The lady responded, "Well, that's okay. Just write it for fifty dollars."

And that was it! The debt was erased, and they knew that lady was their angel sent from God. God had resurrected their financial situation. I want to encourage you to think big when it comes to God meeting your needs. He delights to do the impossible for you.

When my mother was diagnosed with cancer of the liver in 1981, she didn't get healed overnight, but she didn't give up on God or his Word. She had even-now faith! It took longer than we all wanted, but God did the impossible in her life!

Even though God doesn't work on our timetable, I want you to know that he is deeply moved by your situation. When Jesus saw Mary and Martha's heartache, he wept. Jesus is our Great High Priest, and he sympathizes with our weaknesses. Let this sink down in your heart. God loves you, and he is moved by your situation. He knows what is going on in your life and, even when it doesn't seem like anything is moving in your favor, trust that God is working on your behalf.

## Roll Away the Stone

The tombs in Lazarus' day were usually six feet by nine feet and about ten feet tall. They had a circular rock, that looked similar to a wheel, as the door. The rock sat on a groove so the tomb could easily be sealed or opened. When Jesus was ready to raise Lazarus, he told Mary and Martha to roll away the stone. When you think about it, Jesus could have removed it himself, but he didn't. This tells me that there are things God expects us to do in the process of receiving our miracle.

Sometimes there are stones that we must roll away, as they are hindrances to our miracle. We have to be willing to pray, "Father, what is my part? What do you want me to do?"

I was in Atlanta some time ago, and I met a woman named

Laine Lawson Craft. She told me her story, and it blessed me so much. She and her husband live in Mississippi, and they have been in the oil business for a long time. She told me that ten years before, they went broke. Business was down, and they were hardly making it. Even their marriage seemed hopeless.

They are believers, but something wasn't quite right. They started watching my brother Joel on television and decided they needed to be in the atmosphere of faith at Lakewood. So as much as they could, they would book the cheapest flights they could find to come to our Saturday night services. As they sat under Joel's teaching, they recognized they were not really acting on the Word of God as they should. They realized that they needed to work on some things.

So, they began to change the way they did things. Their faith began to grow as they heard the Word of God. They began to listen to and obey God. Laine and her husband Steve realized that they needed to start treating each other better. Their lives began to change as they grew spiritually.

Soon, Laine's husband began feeling a strong urge in his spirit to drill for oil in a place he had drilled more than forty times already! Not one of those forty drills brought up anything. Everyone told him to give up, but now he had a new surge of faith. That even-now faith began to rise up within him. This time when he drilled, he struck oil!

Today, they are prosperous and serving God with all their heart—and God is using them to write books, speak, and minister to others. Laine couldn't give God enough praise! But the key for them was to begin acting on the Word of God.

> *God is not going to do for you what you need to do for him.*

God is not going to do for us

what we need to do for him. God told Noah, "I am going to save you from the flood, but you are going to have to build an ark for me." God said to Moses, "I am going to deliver Israel out of the hand of Egypt, but you are going to have to use the rod I am placing in your hand." God told Naaman, "I will heal you of leprosy, but you have to go and dip seven times in the Jordan River." Naaman almost missed his miracle because he was too proud to obey the prophet. Don't let pride or disobedience keep you from your miracle! Do what God asks you to do.

God is saying to you, "You roll away the stone, and I will take it from there."

## Take Off Your Grave Clothes

When Mary and Martha were willing to do things God's way, they saw the miracle-working power of God in their brother's life. They rolled that stone away, and Jesus stood up and said with a loud voice, "Lazarus, come out!" Lazarus came out of the grave still bound in his grave clothes. What a sight to see!

I want to tell you this: All it takes is one word from God—one supernatural act of God—and your life is changed forever! One moment you can be in a situation that looks like it could never change—and then God intervenes, and in the next moment you are rejoicing over the miracle-working power of God.

God is saying to you: "My miracle-working power is at work in your life. Take off your grave clothes!"

You may have already put your grave clothes on concerning your marriage, your finances, or your health, but God is saying: "Don't pronounce death over your situation! Take off those old grave clothes! Exercise your even-now faith!"

"I am the resurrection and the life," Jesus said. He loves to do the impossible for you. Things may look like they are dying. You may have already placed them in the tomb and covered it with a stone, but Jesus is on the way. Your promise may be three days away, like it was for David after he fought at Ziklag. It may be four days away, like it was for Lazarus, but it is never too late for a miracle.

Don't settle into disappointment. Don't quit, and don't lay down for the enemy to walk all over you. Muster up some of the even-now faith and believe that God raises dead things back to life. Take off those old grave clothes. Take off hopelessness and depression. Put on your garments of praise because God is planning a resurrection for you!

## PRACTICAL APPLICATION

*Encouraging thoughts and scriptures to meditate on:*

- God desires to do the impossible for me. He can do what I cannot do. Matthew 19:26 says, "Jesus looked at them and said, 'With man this is impossible, but with God all things are possible.'"

- Jesus is the resurrection and the life, and he can resurrect the dead things in my life. John 1:25 says, "Jesus said to her, 'I am the resurrection and the life.'"

- God is deeply moved by my situation and he is working in my favor even though I may not see it. Hebrews 4:15 says, "For we do not have a High Priest who is unable to sympathize and understand our weaknesses and temptations, but One who has been tempted [knowing exactly how it feels to be human] in every respect as we are, yet without [committing any] sin" (AMP).

### Practical steps I can take:

- I will have even-now faith knowing that God can do what I cannot do.

- I will roll away any stones by making the necessary changes to cooperate with God.

- I will meditate on the promises of God day and night and be careful to obey his commands.

# 10

# Hold on to Your Seed

⁓

*Those who hear the word, accept it, and bear fruit.*
—Mark 4:20, NKJV

What if I told you that everything you're going through right now has less to do with the answer, breakthrough, or provision you've been praying for and everything to do with the seed God has planted in your heart? As I've been saying, you have a very real enemy who knows the value of what's inside you and his sole mission is to shake it loose and steal it from you. Jesus tells us that Satan desires to have us, to sift us as wheat (Luke 22:31). It is his goal to make sure you do not live the abundant life Jesus died to give you.

The seed within you that helps you live this life is the Word of God (Luke 8:11). Living, breathing, active, sharp, and discerning, God's Word is the catalyst for every transformed life, every healed heart, and every renewed mind. It is the very wisdom of God that helps you know God's plan for your life, how to make the right decisions and choose the right friendships, how to be successful in business, and how to treat people. It tells you how to manage your thought life. The Word of God has the answers you need. Psalm 119:105 says that his word is a lamp to your feet and a light to your path.

We often say that when we are born, we don't come with a manual, but the Bible is just that. It is our instruction manual for navigating life here on earth. It helps us live the victory Jesus won for us on the cross. Psalm 119:18 says that "through your commandments [God's Word], Lord, you have made me wiser than my enemies."

Even more than all of this is the beautiful truth that Jesus is the living Word of God—the Word made flesh (John 1:14). When we abide in Christ, we also abide in his Word—us in him and he in us. Through God and his divine power, we have been given access to "all things that pertain to life and godliness" (2 Pet. 1:3). The more we abide in God and his Word, the more fruitful our lives will be. Our thoughts come to align with his thoughts. We begin to understand his will, and when we pray, we receive what we ask for because we pray his will and his Word. John 15:7 says, "If you remain in me and my words remain in you, ask whatever you wish, and it will be done for you. This is to my Father's glory, that you bear much fruit, showing yourselves to be my disciples."

The Bible is also your key to developing the faith you need to believe God in these times of waiting for his promises to be fulfilled in your life. Hebrews 11:1 says that "faith comes by hearing and hearing by the word of God." You need God's Word to be planted deep in your heart so that you have a firm hold on it and it is not easily pulled loose no matter what challenges come your way.

You may be familiar with Jesus' parable of the seed and the sower found in Mark 4:3–20 and Luke 8.

In this parable, Jesus compared his Word to seed a farmer sows, and our hearts to the ground upon which the seed is sown. Then he uses several examples of how the enemy keeps that seed from taking root and therefore, keeping it from producing a harvest in our lives. These examples point directly to some of the things that keep us from receiving answers to our prayers! This is why I love God's Word. In it, Jesus exposes the enemy's plots, so you gain the advantage.

## Sowing the Seed

As you read the parable of the sower, understand that what Jesus is really talking about is *you* sowing the Word of God in your heart. A seed has to be sown in order for it to produce a harvest. A seed that is never planted will never produce anything. This seed, as we have discovered, is the Word of God, and even though it is alive and powerful and sharper than any two-edged sword, it can sit on your nightstand and never produce anything in your life *until* you do something with it.

This seed has the potential to bring healing and restoration into your life. It has the potential to transform your life, but it will produce nothing until you sow it into your life. So how do you do that? I'm so glad you asked!

The way you sow the Word into your heart is by reading it, hearing it, meditating on it, praying it, and acting on it. When you do these things, faith begins to grow in your heart and produce a great harvest in your life. That harvest could be freedom from an addiction, a financial need met, a physical healing, restoration in your family, a dream come to pass—whatever you are praying.

This is what you must understand. No one can do the sowing for you! You have to take the time and effort to sow the Word into your own heart. Have you ever tried to help someone, but it seems like you are doing all the work? They don't take action themselves. They don't read the Bible for themselves, but they keep coming back to you for more help. This has happened to me before. That person becomes totally dependent on you to encourage and pray for them. It's like pulling a dead horse, because they want you to do for them what they need to do for themselves. They will never gain the victory until they learn to read the Word of God for themselves—until they learn to sow it into their own hearts—because that's when it will begin to grow and produce results in their life.

We will be no different from the person in this example if we aren't proactive about reading, hearing, meditating, and acting on the Word of God. This is how we stay encouraged and full of faith as we wait on the promise, the dream, and the answers to our prayers.

I mentioned earlier that I was born with a crippling disease and that the doctors told my parents I would never walk or talk. They predicted that my parents would have to take care of me the rest of my life. My parents heard what the doctors said, but as they turned to God and began to discover what the Bible says about healing, the seeds of God's truth began to take root in their hearts. Their faith began to grow, and they began praying and speaking the Word over me. That Word produced a harvest of healing in my life. They planted healing seeds and reaped a healing harvest. That's the power of the Word of God!

If you want the Word to work in your life, here is the key: After you sow the seed of the Word into your heart, you must then cultivate that seed just like a farmer does. This means you have to watch over it, protect it, water it, and nurture it—because once you sow the Word in your heart, you have a battle on your hands. In his parable, Jesus mentioned specific things that will try to steal the Word of God out of your heart. We're going to look at those things now. Then we'll talk about how to guard your heart to protect the seed you've sown.

## Tempter, Accuser, Thief

Satan is a thief. We know this. We are not ignorant of his schemes—at least we aim not to be. The Bible says that he comes to steal, kill, and destroy you (John 10:10), that he is a thief and liar, and he is the tempter and accuser (Rev. 12:10). Because you are a child of God, you don't need to play guessing games with the enemy. You need to be sharp and stay sober. Being able to recognize how the enemy comes against your life is a matter of life and death.

Jesus says, "Some people are like seed along the path, where the word is sown. As soon as they hear it, Satan comes and takes away the word that was sown in them" (Mark 4:14–15). In the parable, Jesus likens the birds of prey that ate up the farmer's seed to Satan—our enemy. He says that as soon as the seed is sown into the soil of our hearts—as soon as we receive the Word, either by reading it or hearing it—Satan comes immediately to steal it out of our hearts.

This means that, as soon as you sow the Word in your heart, Satan is on the move. He wants to get it out of you. Why? Because he is afraid of the Word in you. He is afraid of what will happen in you and to you if that Word lands on the fertile places of your heart and begins to take root. His urgency to pluck up that seed should tell you something. It should tell you that Satan is afraid of what the Word will produce in your life. It should tell you that he knows it will expose his lies and take you to a new level. It should tell you he knows that the Word in you will help you overcome the trial you are in right now; Satan knows that if you find out who you really are in Christ Jesus, you can take authority over him in the name of Jesus!

I have come to understand why the devil wants to steal the Word from me—because every time I hold on to the Word of God, like Acts 19:20 says, it grows mightily in me and prevails. The Word in me will give me power to prevail over my circumstances. It will cause me to prevail over sickness and disease. It will help me prevail over discouragement.

I may not prevail overnight, but if I hold on to the Word—whether I feel like it or not—I will prevail. This seed is the eternal Word of God. Has God not said it, and will he not bring it to pass? (See Numbers 23:19.) Oh, yes, he will. Amen, and so be it! I'm not going to let Satan steal my seed!

One thing you need to know is that if he steals our seed, then he steals our faith. And if he steals our faith, he steals our victory. I hope you will not stand by and let that happen. You are much too close to victory for it to end like that. Remember David and how he was just three days away from being king of Israel when he had just come out of the worst trial of his life? Stay in position to reap a victorious harvest. You do this by holding on to your seed.

> *Stay in position to reap a victorious harvest by holding on to the Word of God.*

John 5:4 says, "This is the victory that overcomes the world, even our faith." You see, Satan is after our faith because faith is what moves God to act on our behalf. He knows that when you speak the Word of God with faith in your heart, it's as if God himself were speaking! He knows that when you pray the Word of God in faith, all of heaven stands to attention and the angels hearken to the voice of God's Word.

You must get the revelation that Satan wants to steal your seed. That battle you are fighting is not over the things you are praying for; it is for the Word. You have to hold on to your seed. Don't let it go! Because when you let your seed go, you let your harvest go.

You may be thinking, *How does Satan come to steal from me?* This is what I want to share with you. I want to mention six ways Satan comes to steal the Word of God from you. Again, we cannot be ignorant of how he works to keep us from enjoying every promise God has made in his Word.

*Six Ways Satan Steals the Word of God*

1. Passivity. To be passive means that you don't take any action. You wish Satan would leave you alone and that you didn't have to deal with difficulties. You're always on the defensive, dodging his fiery darts. But you have to get on the offensive and begin to exercise your God-given authority to put the fire out or extinguish those darts.

   You may find yourself behaving like the ostrich. You may have seen how they put their heads in the ground and think they are hiding. The truth is their tail end is exposed and they are still fair game.

   You can't hide from or run from the enemy. You must do as James 4:7 says, "Resist the devil and he will flee from you." You must do something. Resist and refuse Satan's lies because you cannot afford to be passive when it comes to holding on to God's Word.

2. Procrastination. You know what to do, but you put it off. The enemy loves it when you procrastinate in the things of God—when you put off reading the Word and when you put off obeying God. You'd rather sit in front of the television

and feel sorry for yourself instead of resisting the enemy and speaking the Word over your life. Don't wait any longer. No one else can do it for you. Start now!

3. The voice of others. Sometimes we allow people to influence us, discourage us, or talk us out of our dreams. When Kevin and I were praying to have children, someone said to us, "Maybe it's not God's will for you to have children." Those words hit like a dagger, but out of my spirit came the Word that I had planted in my heart. "God makes the barren woman to be a happy mother of children. Children are a blessing from God, and he will not withhold his blessings from us!" I was not going to allow anyone to steal my blessings!

When you know what is at stake, it is your responsibility to not let anyone talk you out of doing what you need to do to get your answer! We talked about pressing through in chapter 5 when we looked at the experience of the woman with the issue of blood. Who can imagine all the terrible things people said to her? She didn't let their words stop her. So, you don't do it either: Don't let anyone talk you out of God's promises.

4. Accusations. Satan will accuse you and tell you that you're not worthy to receive from God or you're not worthy to enjoy God's blessings. Don't buy into that lie. The fact is, we were not worthy—but Jesus made us worthy, and Satan just has to deal with that!

5. Discouragement. Sometimes we get discouraged because things are not happening like we want them to happen. In this state of mind, we tend to give up on the Word, when all the while our harvest is on the way. This is the time to

recognize that the enemy is trying to steal from you. Be on guard and resist the temptation to give up!

6. Doubt. We begin to believe the lies of the enemy over the Word of God. We start to entertain the question, "Did God really say...?" just like Adam and Eve did. We take our eyes off of Jesus and begin to look at our circumstances. Jesus said to his disciples one time, "O you of little faith! Why do you doubt?" I can hear the cry of his heart, "Why do you doubt me?" Doubt your own doubts. Doubt Satan. But don't doubt God!

Many years ago, my dad would hold missions conferences. Our church community would house hundreds of missionaries from all over the world for several days, and he and others would encourage and preach to them. We always fed the missionaries three meals a day, which obviously was a large expense. Well, one year my dad had a desire to pray that God would give the church two cows we could use for beef that would feed all the guests. God placed that desire in him, and he had the faith for it. There was just one problem: Our timing is not always God's timing.

As the conference time drew nearer, nobody showed up with the two cows. We were all saying, "God, where's the beef?" My dad started to get nervous and gave up praying for his two cows. To compensate, we went to the store and bought all the beef we needed.

It wasn't too much later, after we'd conceded to what we saw as reality, that God gave my dad a dream. In the dream, he saw two snakes that had each swallowed something huge. As he looked closer, he could see the outline of a cow inside of each snake. He woke up immediately, and God spoke to his spirit and said, "I want you to know, son, that you let Satan steal your two cows." From that day on, my dad determined that he would never give up and allow Satan to steal from him again.

Don't let Satan steal your cows, your dreams, your breakthrough, your healing, your finances, or your harvest. What God has planted inside you is yours!

## Grow Some Roots!

Jesus taught us in the parable that the trials of life would also come to steal our seed. He said, "Others, like seed sown on rocky places, hear the word and at once receive it with joy. But since they have no root, they last only a short time. When trouble or persecution comes because of the word, they quickly fall away" (Mark 4:17).

You can receive the Word of God with great joy, and yet when trials and persecution come, as Jesus said, some believers quickly fall away. One Bible version says, "You quickly let go of the Word." Can you see that picture? You let go of the powerful seed of the Word of God, the very thing that will help you grow spiritually and experience victory.

Proverbs 24:10 says, "If you faint in the day of adversity, how small is your strength." So we have to grow up in God and learn to develop maturity in order to put down some roots in our lives.

The Word of God helps us become spiritually strong. Hebrews 5:13 talks about growing up in the things of God—and not remaining a baby when it comes to spiritual things. I like how it reads in the Amplified Bible: "For everyone who continues to feed on milk is obviously inexperienced and unskilled in the doctrine of righteousness...for he is a mere infant [not able to talk yet]! But solid food is for the spiritually mature."

Babies need milk at first, but they eventually advance to solid food. And as believers, we need to grow up from that baby stage and mature to where we are feeding on the meat of the Word of God—where you are acquainted with the Word of God and you don't pout and cry all the time because you don't get your way.

I remember when our twin girls were almost one year old, and I had decided to take them off their bottles and switch to sippy cups. Caroline, being the happy-go-lucky child she is, just inspected it and accepted it. But Catherine was different. She's always been a more strong-willed child. She threw that sippy cup as far as she could and crawled over to the refrigerator and pointed to it as if to say, "I want my bottle!"

When I didn't give it to her, she threw a temper tantrum. Instead of giving in to her demands, I walked away and ignored her. She finally realized that she wasn't getting her bottle, so she crawled over to her sippy cup, picked it up, and began drinking.

That's the way it is with us spiritually sometimes. We don't want to grow up. We resist change and growth because we are used to depending on others. But there comes a time when you have to go from the bottle to the sippy cup—from milk to solid food.

You will learn that how you accept the growth process reveals how you will handle the hardships of life. If you are mature and strong, you will realize that your faith is being developed even in the trials. You will not simply procrastinate, be passive, or try to hide from them. You will face them with the strong faith you have built up as you have sown God's Word deep in your heart.

The resistance we build up as we go through the trials of life is very much the same process we apply when trying to build our physical muscles. Every trainer knows that if there is no resistance, then our muscles will not develop.

It's in the trials of life that we grow spiritually and our faith is stretched. It's in these trials that we learn that God is our God, that he answers our prayers, and that he is our faithful friend, who never leaves us or forsakes us.

Most of the time, we want everything to be easy for us, as we came to see in chapter 4. Our flesh wants to take the easy way out. But as I have shared with you, I've learned that the easy way out doesn't get you anywhere. You just repeat the same old cycle. We have to deal with the same old problem until we learn to do what God commanded us to do.

So don't just go through trials; learn to grow through them. This means that you will have to be patient until the harvest comes. Put some roots down in your life. Don't give up, don't blame God, and don't give in to discouragement or have a pity party. I know we like our pity parties, but there are two things wrong with them: No one ever comes to the pity party but you and there are never any refreshments!

Think back to the farmer Jesus uses as an example in his parable. He works very hard and for a long time to till and prepare his soil. Then he sows his seed. His next step is patience. This is the longest step in the process—waiting for the harvest. The farmer has to wait for the seed to germinate and take root. He has to wait for the rain. He has to wait for the plants to mature. He has to be patient in the winter months. Winter is the hardest time to be patient, because it is a period of dormancy—when it seems like absolutely nothing is happening on the outside.

Have you ever been there? Have you ever prayed, and it seemed like nothing was happening? You have sown your seed. You've spoken, prayed, and declared over it. You may have even marched around it seven times like the Israelites marched around Jericho! Yet it still seems like nothing is happening. It seems like God has gone on vacation. This only means that it's wintertime! God is working. You just can't see it—yet! That's why you have to keep walking by faith and not by sight. You can't go by what you see. You must go by what you know. You know the truth, and the truth will set you free.

You see, a farmer knows that the seed is growing underground whether he can see it or not. He doesn't try to dig up the seed to check on it. He doesn't worry about it. He simply waits until the harvest is ready. That's the way God planned the process—it's called seed...time...and harvest. And you just can't rush the process.

Like that farmer, you have to be patient and know that God is working in your life—whether you see it or not. You have to know that God is watching over his Word to fulfill it. God has a plan for you, and he is working out his plan for your life. You can't hurry God's plan. You must be patient and trust God to bring the harvest.

Whenever you are tempted to give up in the trials of life, remember Job. He went through many difficult trials, but he persevered. In the end, remember what God did for Job? He healed him, delivered him, and gave him twice as much as he had before. God brings you out of the trial better than you were before.

> *God brings you out of the trial better than you were before.*

Job's roots went deep, and when your roots go deep, you won't wilt in the day of adversity. You have sustaining power! When your roots go deep, you experience the miracle-working power of God!

## Don't Get Choked

Jesus said in Mark 4:18–19, "Still others, like seed sown among thorns, hear the word; but the worries of this life, the deceitfulness of wealth and the desires for other things come in and choke the word, making it unfruitful." The Message Bible says that this person becomes overwhelmed with worries about all the things they have to do and all the things they want to get. The stress strangles what they heard, and nothing comes of it.

Jesus referred to these weeds as thorns that choke the seed of God's Word in your life. There are three forms in which these thorns show up in our spiritual lives. Jesus named them as the worries of life, the deceitfulness of riches, and the desire for other things. (See Mark 4:18–19.)

Let me ask you this: Do you have any distractions in your life that are choking the Word of God? A distraction is anything that draws your attention away from God, the Word of God, and the things of God. Perhaps you've become so busy that you don't take time to read God's Word. You've begun to find yourself putting off doing the very things that will bring you peace and victory. Perhaps you feel like you are too stressed out to pray. While all of this may be true, what you don't realize is that if you took the time to pray, you wouldn't be so stressed out.

Maybe you spend your time and energy worrying instead of trusting God. Or, maybe you are so consumed with work and getting ahead and obtaining material things that you have lost your first love for God. Maybe you are focusing so much on the dream that you have forgotten the Dream-Giver. Maybe you have a hard time saying no to people. You mean well, but your schedule is so full that it has crowded the Word out of your life. These are distractions that come to steal your seed!

Hebrews 12:1 says, "Let us throw off everything that hinders and the sin that so easily entangles." We need to pray that God will show us anything that is distracting us from him. We can make changes. We can adjust our schedule. We can learn to say no when we know we need to say no. We can evaluate our priorities.

Decide today, right now, that you are going to get rid of any distractions in your life. Decide this very moment that you are not going to allow anything to steal your seed, that you are going to hold on to the promises God has given you.

At the end of his parable, Jesus said, "Those who hear the word, accept it, and bear fruit," or as I like to say, they bear a harvest. And not just any harvest. The Message translation says, "But the seed planted in the good earth [that's you and me] represents those who hear the Word, embrace it, and produce a harvest beyond their wildest dreams."

> *God can produce a harvest beyond your wildest dreams!*

Maybe your harvest will be a harvest of restoration or physical healing. Maybe it will be supernatural favor or a new home. Whatever it is—if you will hold on to your seed—God will give you a harvest beyond your wildest dreams!

I hope the phrase *hold on to your seed* is engraved into your spirit after reading this chapter and that you will never forget it. Switch it around and make it your declaration when the enemy, the trials of life, the voices of others, doubt, or accusations come and try to steal the Word out of your heart. Declare it now, "I will hold on to my seed!"

## PRACTICAL APPLICATION

### *Encouraging thoughts and scriptures to meditate on:*

- The Word of God has the answers I need. Psalm 119:105 says, "Your word is a lamp to my feet and a light to my path."

- The Word of God is like a seed that must be planted in my heart and it has the potential to transform my life. Mark 4:20 says, "But the seed planted in the good earth represents those who hear the Word, embrace it, and produce a harvest beyond their wildest dreams."

- The Word of God will help me stay encouraged and full of faith as I wait on the promise, the dream, and the answers to my prayers. Hebrews 11:1 says, "Now faith is the substance of things hoped for, the evidence of things not seen."

### *Practical steps you can take:*

- I will sow the Word of God into my heart daily.

- I will not allow Satan to steal the Word of God from me.

- I will be patient until my harvest comes.

# 11

# Be Joyful Now

‿

*Always be joyful. Keep on praying. No matter what happens, always be thankful, for this is God's will for you who belong to Christ Jesus.*

—1 Thessalonians 5:16–17, NLT

Often, in life's most difficult moments, we may begin to wonder if God is trying to tell us something. We wonder if the difficult times have come to wake us up or to alert us that we need to realign with God in some way. We may pray, asking God, "What is your will for me in this situation?" Well, 1 Thessalonians 5:16–17 doesn't mince words: "Always be joyful. Keep on praying. No matter what happens, always be thankful, for this is God's will for you" (NLT). It may be hard to imagine being joyful with the challenges you are living through right now, but this is it. Being full of joy is God's will for you always.

When you think about it, attitude is everything. Proverbs 23:7 says, "As a man thinks in his heart, so is he." Your attitude affects everything—from your own life, your atmosphere, and even others.

You've probably heard the saying, "If Mama isn't happy, no one is happy!" Your attitude sets the tone for how you and others around you will respond to the ups and downs that naturally happen in life.

Our parents set the tone of Lakewood Church sixty-two years ago. When people walk into our church, they experience an atmosphere of love, joy, peace, and the presence of God. They can sense it, and it's wonderful to experience. This is exactly what our parents intended. They said that Lakewood would be a church that loves all people—a church that preaches the Word, worships God, and believes that God is a miracle-working God. And we continue to carry that on.

People tell us all the time, "When I stepped into the church for the first time, I felt the love of God. I felt the presence of God." It's amazing how we can set a tone and atmosphere, actually creating our own environment.

Have you ever walked into a place or someone's home and felt tension or anger? You can cut it with a knife. It's uncomfortable, and you don't want to stay in that environment.

Emotions like joy or sadness create an atmosphere. If your friend or loved one is sad, you feel and sense that sadness. If someone is afraid, that creates an anxious atmosphere. Have you noticed how if you're happy, everything is good? But if you're grumpy or angry, it's like you're mad at the world. If you're sad, everything in your life looks miserable, grim, and hopeless. Even other people's lives look bad to you. Your emotions set a tone and dictate your mood. But through the Holy Spirit, we have the power to choose our attitude and set our own atmosphere.

*Atmosphere* is defined as "the special mood or character associated with a place."[6] Atmosphere is important. Your home should be

---

[6] Dictionary.com, s.v. "atmosphere," https://www.dictionary.com/browse/atmosphere?s=t.

a place of peace and joy and the presence of God. We may think that our circumstances dictate our atmosphere and our life, but they don't. We do that by the things we choose to say and do. So, let's not lie down and allow circumstances and the enemy to dominate our lives and our joy level. We need to recognize the part we play.

## Choosing Joy

Most of the time, our attitude is a decision we make, and sometimes we need an attitude adjustment. Just like we may tell our children, we may have to tell ourselves, "Lose the attitude!" or "Watch the attitude!"

Of course, this does not mean that you will wake up happy all the time. No, most of the time I wake up groggy. I am hitting the snooze button. I am reaching for my coffee.

There are some people who do wake up happy—like my husband. When Kevin wakes us, he is wide awake, happy, and energetic. Not me! I am still walking around the house with my eyes shut, feeling my way around. It's in these early-morning moments just upon waking that your mind can be bombarded with negative thoughts. So before you get out of bed, you can make some decisions to put your focus on what you can be glad and thankful about.

I have made it a practice to talk to the Lord before I even get out of bed in the morning. I express my love and appreciation to him. I always point out the things I am grateful for because I want to start my day with a thankful heart even though I may be facing some difficult situations.

Choosing joy in the midst of worry, discouragement, and fear is not always easy. If we allow our circumstances and what people do or say to us to dictate our emotions, we could be sad and down all the time. I am not saying that there won't be times of sadness and sorrow in our lives. What I am saying is that life has a tendency to pull us down on an everyday basis if we are not careful to guard our attitude and atmosphere. We can have joy even in the valleys of life.

I think sometimes we get in a rut of thinking, *When I get through this trial, I will be happy and at peace. When my child starts serving God, I will be joyful.* How about being joyful now? How about enjoying your life and all the blessings you have now?

After living through my own trials, I decided to study what the Bible has to say about joy. In the Hebrew language, *joy* means "cheerfulness, gladness, and a calm delight."[7] That's a lot different than happiness, which is based solely on your happenings or circumstances. The joy of the Lord is an inner joy, a calm delight that only comes from trusting God. We may not be happy with what we're going through, but we can walk in the joy God gives us in the meantime.

> *The joy of the Lord is an inner joy, a calm delight that only comes from trusting God.*

Jesus modeled this so well for us. The Bible says that he was full of joy through the Holy Spirit (Luke 10:21). And every person Jesus touched became joyful, including the disciples. Acts 13:52 says that they too were filled with joy and with the Holy Spirit. They had hardships like we do. They were persecuted because they served Jesus. But they had the joy of the Lord, and they spread that joy wherever they went.

It's important to understand that being a Christian isn't always

---

[7] BibleHub.com, s.v. "*chara*," https://biblehub.com/greek/5479.htm.

easy, but it doesn't mean you have to be somber all the time. The kingdom of God, which we have been translated into, is all about joy and peace and being in right standing with God. You see, God delivered us from the kingdom of darkness into a kingdom of joy, as it says in Romans 14:17: "For the kingdom of God is not a matter of eating and drinking, but of righteousness, peace and joy in the Holy Spirit."

Jesus carried our griefs and pain on the cross so that we could walk in his joy and live an abundant life. He promised to turn our sorrow into dancing and our mourning into joy!

## Overflowing with Joy

The unspeakable joy Jesus demonstrated is available to us. We can either suppress it or release it in our lives. Jesus said in John 15:10–11, "When you obey my commandments, you remain in my love, just as I obey my Father's commandments and remain in his love. I have told you these things so that you will be filled with my joy. Yes, your joy will overflow!" Jesus wants you to be filled to overflowing with his joy!

We will have seasons of ups and downs, but we can be filled with joy by the Holy Spirit. What a blessing it is to serve such a good God! Do you know what the apostle Paul said in 2 Corinthians 7:4? He said, "In all our tribulation, I am overflowing with joy." No matter what we go through we can overflow with joy and an inner calm that only God can give.

Obeying God is vital to our being able to overflow with joy. In the verse we read from John 15 just above, Jesus said, "If you obey My commands…your joy will be complete." Every day we need to make the decision to walk in obedience to God, to obey his Word and his commands. Disobedience steals our joy and peace. Sometimes we think we can ignore some of God's commands and get by, but disobedience always costs us something. It always catches up with us. It steals our blessings and gets us into difficult situations. It never ever pays to disobey God.

When you are in sin, you have this constant burden on you—the burden of guilt, shame, and condemnation. You know that you are not living a life that is pleasing to God. But Jesus said that his commands are not a burden to us. His yoke is easy, and his burden is light.

So if you are in a compromising place, I encourage you to make a change today. The Bible says to flee from evil. When you repent of your sin, God will freely forgive you. He will cleanse you from all unrighteousness and then you will enjoy his best.

## Joy's Healing Power

Walking in the joy of the Lord has benefits that include much more than a good mood you feel. God is so sovereign. As our Creator, he knows all the things that make for a good life for his children—mind, body, and spirit. We cannot underestimate the life-giving nature of God's commands. When we come to understand the connection between obedience, joy, and our physical life, we can see how God intends only good for us.

Your joyful attitude affects your physical body in a positive way. Nehemiah 8:10 says, "The joy of the Lord is your strength." Proverbs 17:22 says, "A merry heart does good like a medicine." Joy acts like a medicine and affects every area of our lives. Studies show that smiling makes us look younger and more attractive—who wouldn't start smiling more just for that benefit![8] Laughter releases endorphins in our brain, and those endorphins help our bodies fight diseases by relieving stress, elevating our mood, boosting our immune systems, and lowering our blood pressure. Smiling and laughter—physical expressions of joy—release healing power!

Smiling is contagious and when we feel good, other people around us feel good. You never know who needs a smile around you. You are a carrier of the joy of the Lord. Most people have no idea what it's like to have true joy. But you do! Spread joy and its healing power. Don't keep it to yourself.

Proverbs 15:15 says, "The cheerful heart has a continual feast no matter what the circumstances" (AMP). This reminds me of what Psalm 23 says—that God prepares a table for me in the presence of my enemies. No matter what the enemy is trying to do to us, we can sit down at God's table and have a feast because we know that the victory is ours! Let the enemy look on—but we are going to feast at the table of God's healing and deliverance.

Your choice to smile throughout your day reinforces your trust in God. It's a message to yourself that even though you don't quite see how God will work everything out, you know he will. You know the victory is yours, so why not praise God in advance? It will do your heart good.

When you wake up, make the decision, and say, "I am going to put a smile on my face today! I am going to be thankful and spread God's joy! If this feels like more than you can manage and you find

---

[8] Mark Stibich, PhD, "Top Ten Reasons You Should Smile Every Day," VeryWellMind .com, February 4, 2020, https://www.verywellmind.com/top-reasons-to-smile-every -day-2223755.

yourself lacking in joy, believe me, I have been there. Let me give you a checklist of five things that you can work on.

## How to Maintain the Joy of the Lord

*1. Remember who is the true Source of joy.*

Sometimes we get caught up in our circumstances and what we don't have—and we completely lose our joy. But you have to stop and ask yourself, "What is true and lasting joy?" It is having a personal relationship with the Lord Jesus Christ. Only he can give you true joy and fulfillment.

You may not have much on this earth, but if you have Jesus—you have it all! On the other hand, you can have everything this world has to offer—but if you don't have Jesus, you will never experience true and lasting joy. Jesus is our joy! He is our silver and our gold. He is our pearl of great price! He is our treasure found in the field. (See Matthew 14:44–45.)

We have to be careful that we don't lose our joy and become ungrateful because we don't see our prayers answered right away—or because things aren't going our way. Let's keep our priorities in order. Jesus said that we should not allow "the deceitfulness of riches or the desires for other things come in and choke the word" in your life (Mark 4:19). Let's not be deceived into thinking that one day—when we obtain this or that or when our circumstances are different—we will finally be full of joy. No. We can overflow with joy now because Jesus lives in us and you can't get any better than that.

We have so much to be joyful about! Jesus said that we should rejoice because our names are written in heaven. Rejoice because our sins are forgiven. Then finally Jesus said that we can rejoice because great is our reward in heaven. This world is not our home. We have eternity to spend with the Lord—where there will be no pain, no sorrow, and no more tears!

*2. Don't neglect spending time with the Lord every day.*

Psalm 16:11 reminds us that in God's presence is fullness of joy. We have to stay connected with our source of joy. He is the vine, and we are the branches. Apart from him we can do nothing, so stay hooked up with the vine every day. (See John 15.)

I watched my parents spend time with the Lord every morning, whether it was in their recliners in the family room, or when my dad would read the Bible and pray in the backyard under our big oak tree.

When I was about ten years old, my parents gave me what I call a grown-up Bible with my name on it. My father said to me, "Lisa, the Bible is God speaking to you. Read it every day and God will speak to you." And then he added, "Don't be afraid to mark in your Bible and underline scriptures. Talk to God out of your heart because he is listening."

My father was right. The Bible has become my constant companion. It brings wisdom, encouragement, and joy to my life. When I am discouraged, I pick up the Bible and read the Psalms. If you want God to speak to you, then start reading the Bible because it is God's Word and will for your life. If you want to touch and feel God, then touch and handle the Word of God. John 1:1 says, "In the beginning was the Word, and the Word was with God, and the Word was God."

As you make God a priority in your life, you will be transformed in your thinking, you will grow spiritually, and you will not allow circumstances to dictate your joy level. And let me warn you: As you make this your discipline, there will be days when you think you are not getting anything out of the Word, but don't allow that to stop you. You are putting the everlasting, incorruptible Word of the living God in your spirit, and it is making a difference whether you feel it or not. When you put the Word in you, it will come out of you in your time of need.

### 3. Don't allow people to steal your joy.

You know you can get up in the morning and have an awesome time with the Lord. You can be full of joy as you get ready for your day. But you can take one step out of your door, and you will have a dozen reasons to be offended and lose your joy. Somebody will say something negative to you, or cut you off in traffic and you spill your coffee all over your clothes. That's actually happened to me!

If we are not careful, we will allow these things to ruin our day and steal our joy. Proverbs 19:11 says, "A person's wisdom yields patience; it is to one's glory to overlook an offense."

Some of our family members went with my brother Joel to Las Vegas—not to gamble but for one of our Night of Hope events. While we were there, we took some pastors out to dinner. We were at a nice restaurant in the hotel that had these beautiful water fountains. They were huge, and they moved in sequence as if they were dancing. The windows were open, and it was a gorgeous sight. We weren't sitting by the windows, but our view was clear.

We were all talking when, all of a sudden, I felt this huge rush of water pounding on my head. It was so strong that it shocked me for a moment! Then I realized that one of the fountains had malfunctioned, and it was gushing water on no one else's table but ours!

We were all drenched and ran out of the restaurant trying to escape the deluge! It looked like we had gone swimming! We gathered in the lobby and, after the shock of it, we all started cracking up. We could have been mad, but we chose to laugh about it. After all, it was hilarious, and what were the odds that the fountain would hit only us?

Sure, our clothes, purses, and shoes were soaking wet. Yes, we had to change clothes and redo our hair. We were also late to an event and had to skip dinner. The strange thing about it is that the restaurant employees didn't even seem to care. But that's life! And we can get mad and frustrated or be joyful in all circumstances as the Bible teaches us.

Every day we have to choose to let go of those offenses. We have to stop and determine that we are not going to let anyone or anything steal our joy. We must do what Colossians 3:12 says: Clothe ourselves with compassion, kindness, humility, gentleness, and patience. We can bear with one another and forgive each other when we are offended. Doing these things will help you maintain your joy.

*4. Walking in joy is a choice we have to make daily.*

Nehemiah 8:10 says, "Do not grieve, for the joy of the Lord is your strength." It's a choice we all have to make. We have to say, "I am not going to worry over this situation. I'm not going to be discouraged. I choose to walk in the joy of the Lord!"

The apostle Paul said it this way in Philippians 4:6, "Rejoice in the Lord always. I will say it again: Rejoice!" We have to remind ourselves to rejoice sometimes!

I heard someone say, "We rejoice by choice!"

*Rejoice by choice!*

When we choose joy over sorrow and discouragement, the blessings of God kick in. The joy of the Lord rises up in our spirits and floods our whole being. Feelings follow your choices. When you choose joy, the *feelings* of joy will follow!

David said in Psalm 27:5–6, "In the day of trouble...I will sacrifice with shouts of joy; I will sing and make music to the Lord." Sometimes you have to offer the sacrifice of joy. It's a sacrifice to put aside your feelings and worship the Lord, but the rewards outweigh the sacrifices. I have had to do this many times in my life.

One time, when I was experiencing anxiety attacks, I had to pull myself out of bed every morning. I didn't feel like getting out of bed, but I did. I would read my Bible and pray and not feel any different. Still I refused to give up. I made the decision to sing to the Lord with shouts of joy. I would worship the Lord radically—whether I felt like it or not. I even made a long list of scriptures on joy and read them aloud to myself several times a day. Some days I would think, *This is not working! I still feel the same!* But I know that the Word of God is true, and as I continued, healing and joy returned to me.

There are times when you have to stir up the joy in your heart. Psalm 30:5 says, "Weeping may endure for a night, but joy comes in the morning." When you obey God, joy comes! When you *choose* to rejoice, joy comes! You may be going through a dark time, but I want you to know that joy comes in the morning! The joy of the Lord is your strength!

I do want to say this: If you're going through a season of depression or panic attacks, make sure you talk to your physician, surround yourself with friends who will support you, and talk to a counselor, but please don't isolate yourself. There is absolutely no shame in getting medical help and trusting God to see you through at the same time.

When I was having anxiety attacks, I did everything I could spiritually and medically, as well as lightening my workload. I realized that I had overstressed my body and I had to get more balance in my life. During that time, the Word of God was my strength to not give up and keep moving forward.

*5. If you need joy, then bring joy to someone else.*

There are times when you make an effort to go out of your way to bless people. It may take great sacrifices on your part. You may not feel like it, but you do it anyway. It helps get your mind off of yourself when you do something for someone else. Be a giver because whatever you sow into someone else's life is going to come back to you.

You can volunteer at your church, help a neighbor in need, write notes of encouragement to people, or take the time to pray for friends or loved ones. There are many opportunities to be a blessing to others.

When I have been down and discouraged, I would go see someone in the hospital or call a person to encourage them. There were times I would help feed homeless people during holidays. What I found is that all of these things brought joy to my heart. It actually got my mind off of my circumstances and my own needs. Joy came as I served others.

As you sow joy and encouragement into people, you will reap joy.

## Put on Joy and See God's Salvation

Through all the adversity I have faced, I have learned I have to make a deliberate choice to stir up joy in my life, to radically worship and praise God. Psalm 50:23 says, "He who brings an offering of praise and thanksgiving honors and glorifies Me; and he who orders his way aright [who prepares the way that I may show him], to him I will demonstrate the salvation of God." When we offer the sacrifice of praise and thanksgiving to God, we are actually paving the way for our deliverance!

As I praised God through the hard times, he rescued me out of that horrible pit of despair. He gave me a new song and exchanged my spirit of heaviness for a garment of praise. God will do this for you too.

When you choose to put on joy and praise God even when things aren't going your way at the moment, you are paving the way for your freedom, healing, and deliverance! Ephesians 4:21–23 teaches us that we are to be made new in the attitude of our minds: "You were taught, with regard to your former way of life, to put off your old self, which is being corrupted by its deceitful desires; to be made new in the attitude of your minds; and to put on the new self, created to be like God in true righteousness and holiness."

Our attitudes should line up with the Word of God and who God says we are! I like what Joyce Meyer says: "You can be pitiful or powerful, but you can't be both!" We are not a pitiful people! We are powerful because we have the Holy Spirit in us. We are full of hope because Christ Jesus is our hope of glory. We are full of joy because God has given us an inner joy that the world cannot give us. So let's act like it! Let's renew our minds with the Word of God until we put on the joy of the Lord, which gives us strength to endure these difficult times.

Is your attitude "My situation will never change; bad things always happen to me"? Or is your attitude full of joyful expectation: "I know God is helping me! I trust him. God is a good God and I'm going to enjoy my life today! I'm not putting off joy for another time"?

Let's not allow oppression and discouragement to hang around us. Like David, start praising and thanking God in the midst of your trials. Keep the right attitude. Isaiah 61:3 talks about taking off the spirit of heaviness and putting on the garment of praise. You have to take off some things and you have to put on some things. Take off a negative attitude and replace it with a grateful attitude. God has given you that choice.

The Bible also teaches us to put on the Lord Jesus Christ. Romans 13:14 says, "Clothe yourself with the presence of the Lord Jesus Christ. And don't let yourself think about ways to indulge your evil desires." You can usher in the presence of God with the right attitude.

You may say, "I can't help how I feel!" This may be true, but you can help how you respond to your feelings. Are you going to just go with the flow and allow your emotions to dominate you, or are you going to do some taking off and putting on?

Choosing to change your attitude, shift your atmosphere, and set the tone for how you will respond to the season you are in is an act of faith. Faith takes action. Faith isn't moved by what it sees, but by the Word of God! When you put on the joy of the Lord, your atmosphere shifts, and oppression, heaviness, hurt, weakness, problems, negative emotions and feeling, and even your circumstances have no power over you.

## PRACTICAL APPLICATION

*Encouraging thoughts and scriptures to meditate on:*

- I am full of joy by the Holy Spirit. Luke 10:21 says, "At that time Jesus, full of joy through the Holy Spirit."

  Acts 13:52: "And the disciples were continually filled [throughout their hearts and souls] with joy and with the Holy Spirit."

- Jesus is my source of true lasting joy. Nehemiah 8:10 says, "Don't be dejected and sad, for the joy of the Lord is your strength!"

- Jesus desires for me to overflow with joy. John 15:11 says, "When you obey my commandments, you remain in my love, just as I obey my Father's commandments and remain in his love. I have told you these things so that you will be filled with my joy. Yes, your joy will overflow!"

### *Practical steps I can take:*

- I will stay connected to God, my source of joy, by spending time reading the Word of God.

- I will not allow people or circumstances to steal the joy of the Lord from my heart.

- I choose joy and I will make it a point to bring joy to others.

# 12

# Get Your Fight Back

❦

*I have set before you life and death, blessings and curses. Now*
*choose life.*

—Deuteronomy 30:19

Many times, in the midst of the battles of life, we forget who we are
in Christ and that God is fighting our battles for us. Perhaps you've
been battling for peace in the midst of your storm, for joy to show up
in your morning, or for breakthrough, healing, or freedom to reign.
The enemy has been wearing you down, and somewhere along the
way you switched into survival mode. Dreaming, hoping, and imag-
ining God's best for you as his child got put on the back burner so
you could manage enough strength to make it to the end of each day.
You've succumbed to the tyranny of the urgent and seeing beyond it
seems impossible. You hardly recognize yourself anymore.

The place between the promise and its fulfillment can be a difficult place. It is challenging; I know this so well. You may have grown
weary, but I pray that the words on the pages of this book have been
just the spiritual motivation you need to get back in the fight.

We've talked about doing the right thing the first time around and not giving in to the temptation to take the easy way out. And when you don't know what to do, you know now to go humbly and directly to your source for whatever direction and strategy you need. You know how to shake off the things the enemy tries to attach to you to keep you bound to fear and hopelessness. You've learned the necessity of passing the test that came with the trial, and that even when your dream seems dead, it is never too late for a resurrection. You know how to tap into the joy of the Lord and establish an atmosphere of praise and worship, where God is magnified and your problems are not.

These lessons are all so much about the choices we make in the darkest, most difficult of times—choices that God, through the power of his Spirit, can give us the strength to make. There's one more choice I want to talk to you about. I think it will be one that brings together all that we've discussed so far. It will enable you to keep hopes high that what you are praying or believing for is on the way. When you make this choice, you will feel more stable and secure. You will see yourself as victorious. What am I talking about? I'm talking about your choice to be a victim, or to be a victor—when you know that no one can steal or even alter your blessings or destiny.

Remember that Proverbs 2:7 says, "God holds victory in store for the upright." God has wired you for victory, you are more than a conqueror, and you always triumph in Christ Jesus. Victory is your God-given DNA! Don't forget it, and don't forget that God has also given you free will. While many may want to live a life of victory, everyone does not choose it.

In Deuteronomy 30:19–20, God makes the choice clear—life or death, victim or victor. He says:

*I call heaven and earth as witnesses against you today, that I have set before you life and death, the blessing and the curse; therefore, you shall choose life in order that you may live, you and your descendants, by loving the Lord your God, by obeying His voice, and by holding closely to Him; for He is your life [your good life, your abundant life, your fulfillment] and the length of your days.* (AMP)

Choosing life or choosing death—it is a choice you make. No one else can make that choice for you. So, how do you do that? You choose life by loving the Lord, obeying his voice, and holding closely to him, knowing he will vindicate you and direct your steps into your destiny. So what this looks like in the midst of trials or mistreatment is you making the decision and saying, "God, I choose life! I'm going to keep loving you and obeying you. I'm not going to blame you—I'm going to trust you. I'm staying close to you. I'm NOT going to allow anyone to steal my blessing or destiny."

I think about Abraham. He had a nephew named Lot and he treated him with great kindness. When their family and flocks had grown too large to remain together, Abraham graciously gave Lot the first choice—the first pick of the land. Instead of honoring Abraham, Lot chose the best part of the land. But Abraham didn't let that move him. He kept the right attitude and ended up blessed and successful. Even when people try to steal from you—that doesn't change God's blessing on your life!

Joseph was a victim of jealousy and his brothers sold him into slavery at the age of seventeen. He was mistreated and put in prison, but again, he chose life. He chose God's way. Neither his brothers nor his captors could keep him from his destiny to rule and reign over Egypt.

> *When people try to push you down and keep you from your destiny, God will always lift you up.*

When people try to push you down and keep you from your destiny, God will always lift you up.

If you are dealing with a victim mentality in certain parts of your life, then you need to uproot those wrong thoughts and work on developing a victor mentality. You have to reverse what you're saying and how you're thinking and acting.

Do you ever catch yourself saying negative things like, "I never get a break!" "Why does this always happen to me?" "I always have one problem after another!"

I knew someone who said to me many times, "Every time I go to a restaurant, I get the worst service. It never fails."

Finally, I said to him, "It's always going to happen as long as you think like that and talk like that." How this person looked forward to their dining-out experience is a subtle form of victim mentality.

We really need to silence and defeat the victim mentality within us, so that we can live with a victor mentality.

## Overcome the Victim Mentality

According to psychologists, the victim mentality has become classified as a personality disorder because it is so prevalent. Having acquired or learned this personality trait, a person with a victim mentality tends to regard themselves as a victim of the negative actions of others. They tend to think, speak, and act as if that were the case—even in the absence of clear evidence.[9] It's a learned pat-

---

[9] "The Victim Mentality—What It Is and Why You Use It," *Counselling Blog*, HarleyTherapy .co.uk, April 26, 2016, https://www.harleytherapy.co.uk/counselling/victim-mentality.htm.

tern of thinking. And if it's learned, it can be unlearned! This is why we must renew our minds in the Word of God daily.

Someone who has a victim mentality believes that their success or failure depends on what others do, how others treat them, or what their circumstances are.[10] The truth is that no person can control your life or destiny. The Bible says that God opens doors for you that no one can shut. Proverbs 21:30 says, "There is no wisdom, no insight, no plan that can succeed against the Lord."

Now bad things do happen to good people, and just because bad things happened to you does not mean you are bad. Just because your spouse walked out on you doesn't mean you are a bad spouse. Someone may have mistreated, betrayed, or sexually, physically, or emotionally abused you. You may have secrets no one else knows— secrets about things done to you or things you may have done in response—and because of these things you may feel that God couldn't possibly approve of you. You may feel that if anyone ever found out about these things, you would not be able to do anything with your life. But let me tell you, you are not disqualified from God's love, from your destiny, and from being able to live life to its fullest. Yes, you may have been victimized, but victory is still in your DNA.

A few years ago, I was speaking at a women's event in another state. After one of the services, I was signing my book for people and visiting with them. One lady asked me to pray for her friend who was depressed. She said, "My friend told me she would meet me here for the event, but I called her home and her mother told me she is in bed depressed."

I don't normally do this, but I felt an urgency to say, "Get your friend on the phone, and I will pray with her."

Surprised, she called the lady and gave me her phone. Her friend

---

[10] Ibid.

answered and I said, "Hello, I am the speaker at the women's event and your friend asked me to pray for you."

There was a pause and then she said, "You're the speaker?"

I said, "Yes, I am, and I really feel like you need to come to the next service. I believe God will help you and encourage you."

She said, "I will be there!"

After the second service, I was greeted by both of the ladies. One of them said, "I am the one you called on the phone."

I gave her a big hug and told her I was so glad she got out of bed and came to church.

She said, "Lisa, when you spoke today, something happened to me. I feel totally free of depression, and I am so thankful to God!"

You see, this woman had been through some difficult times. She was hurting, but by the simple action of getting out of bed and out of her house and coming into a place of corporate worship, she was able to get the encouragement she needed to get her fight back and see herself as a victor.

Romans 8:38–39 tells us that nothing "shall be able to separate us from the love of God." There is nothing you could ever do, no shame that could ever be cast upon you that will keep God from loving you. You do not have to go around feeling like a victim and like you don't deserve good things. Negative things happen to every one of us, but that doesn't change the fact that God wired you for victory. It doesn't change the fact that God has a plan and purpose for you. You have to get your fight back and remember who you are in Christ and who you belong to.

The first thing you need to do to get there is to identify any areas where you may be thinking like a victim instead of like a victor. What are you saying and how are you believing that is causing the victim mentality to rule your life? One thing victims do is view trials as defeat right from the beginning. They may say, "I'm a victim because

I'm going through something." They have a defeatist attitude. Victors, on the other hand, know that trials are a part of life. In John 16:33, Jesus said, "In this life you will have trouble, tribulation, distress, and frustration, but be of good cheer." He is saying to you, "I have overcome the world, and you will overcome that victim mentality."

> Victims tend to constantly say, "Why me? Why do I get all the bad breaks?"
> Victors say, "Lord, help me get through this."

> Victims blame others much of the time.
> Victors trust God for provision, restoration, and vindication.

> Victims rely on people for their contentment.
> Victors rely on God because he is their source.

> Victims live from the place of fear.
> Victors live from the place of faith.

> Victims have a negative self-image in many areas.
> Victors see themselves through God's eyes.

> Victims complain a lot.
> Victors have a grateful and thankful attitude.

> Victims feel powerless.
> Victors live by faith, not allowing their feelings to dictate their lives.

> Victims see themselves as weak.
> Victors see themselves as strong in the Lord.

Victims remain in the same thought pattern and the same cycle, but victors are constantly renewing their minds in the Word of God. They are always growing and learning. Victims can be very critical, but victors see the good in people and the good in situations. They could be going through the worst trial, and say, "Well, you know what? I know it's not good. I don't like it. But God said he would take me from glory to glory. My days will get brighter and brighter."

Having our minds transformed from a victim mentality to a victor mentality does not nullify how we feel or downplay what's happening to us. It's shifting away from a limiting and defeating thought process that works against the good things God wants to do in our lives. Victim mentality leaves us bitter, stuck in the past, and expecting the worse. A victor mentality helps us move forward and upward, expecting God's best.

## Know Who You Are

Many years ago, after going through an unwanted divorce, I kept asking the Lord, "Why is this happening to me? Why do I have to go through this? I have served you all my life!" I was stuck in the "why me?" phase and thinking like a victim, because it was a hard time.

I'll never forget what the Lord said to me: "Lisa, stop asking why and realize that you have an enemy who wants to steal from you. He wants to destroy you. He is your real enemy, and I have given you power over him in the name of Jesus!"

God is always right. I was fighting the wrong enemy. His correction that day helped me get my fight back. I stopped asking why and started resisting the lies of Satan. I realized that I was in a fight for my life and destiny, and Satan was not going to win. He wasn't going to keep me in that victim mentality.

We had a German shepherd dog named Scooter growing up. He was the king of the hill in our neighborhood. My dad would take him on walks and be so proud of him. At this one corner, there was a cat that was afraid of Scooter. Every time, Scooter would chase that cat, and the cat would barely escape up a tree. My dad thought, *One day that cat is going to be in big trouble!*

Well, one day, something did happen. Scooter ran after that cat like every other day, but this time the cat didn't run. Instead, he rose up like he was going to attack Scooter—with claws out. All of a sudden, Scooter made a rapid U-turn and ran from the cat. Our brave dog ran from a cat that was much smaller than him! My dad was so embarrassed for Scooter!

Looking back, we realized that cat must have been going to Lakewood Church. He found out who he was in Christ! All joking aside, what happened? The cat was tired of being tormented by Scooter! He took a stand against him.

Let me ask you: When are you going to take a stand against the enemy's plans in your life? When are you going to say no to him? He has no power over you.

Jesus said, "I give you power over ALL the power of the enemy and nothing shall by any means hurt you!" Stop allowing the enemy to torment you! Get your fight back just like that cat!

Genesis 27:40 says, "When you decide to break free—YOU will break the yoke from YOUR neck." When you decide you've had enough—you will break free! You will move forward into your new season! Sometimes we are waiting on God—when he is waiting on us to walk in our God-given authority! Don't settle for anything less than God's best for your life!

Satan will make you feel like a

> *Sometimes we are waiting on God—when he is waiting on us to walk in our God-given authority!*

victim as long as you allow him to. But you must push back and believe what God says about you. You are a victor! You are who God says you are, and this is what his Word says:

*You are blessed with every spiritual blessing (Ephesians 1:3).*

God has equipped you with everything you need to live an abundant life. No one can curse you. No one can stop God's plans for you. A friend of mine told me that he had a friend who was mad at him and tried to put a curse on him. The lady was involved in the occult, but my friend is a believer. This woman tried to curse him with sickness using certain rituals. My friend was not affected or afraid because he knew God had blessed him and no one could curse him. In fact, the lady herself ended up very sick and had to go to the hospital. No matter what people try to speak over you, you have God's blessings on your life!

*You are chosen by God (Ephesians 1:4).*

You have been hand-selected by God himself. The Amplified Bible says: "You have been chosen and appointed beforehand according to the purpose of Him who works everything in agreement with the counsel and design of His will" (vv. 4–5).

If you will obey God, listen to his voice, and walk closely with him, he will bring everything into agreement with his design and his will. God hasn't changed his purpose and design for you just because of what someone did.

*You are adopted as a child of God (Ephesians 1:5).*

His royal blood runs through your veins. You have his DNA. God is your heavenly Father. Jesus is your Lord and Savior. If anyone wants to touch you, they have to get past God first!

If you don't like the way you were born the first time, you can be born again.

*You are redeemed (Ephesians 1:7).*

Jesus paid the price to buy you back from sin and the power of Satan. You no longer belong to the kingdom of darkness. You have been translated into the kingdom of God. You've been teleported!

*You are forgiven (Ephesians 1:7).*

Your past has been deleted, and your slate is clean. You are a new creation in Christ Jesus. You have been given a do-over! You have a new start with a new heart. Nothing from your past can hold you back.

*You are marked with the Holy Spirit (Ephesians 1:13).*

The Amplified Bible says, "You have been stamped with the seal of the Holy Spirit as owned and protected by God." The anointing of the Holy Spirit remains in you. You have his strength, grace, and ability working in you.

*You have been lavished with God's amazing grace (Ephesians 1:7).*

*Lavished* implies generous and extravagant quantities. Some of us need more grace than others—and that's okay!

None of this sounds like a victim mentality to me! When you know who you really are, you get your fight back. You will know what is yours and what is not. God has stored up a great inheritance for you, his child.

Ephesians 1 continues laying out all that comes with your identity in Christ, as it further reveals that God wants you to have a spirit of wisdom and revelation, which cannot coexist with a victim mentality (v. 17). This revelation is about an ever-increasing understanding of who God is. It's a revelation that, as you are created in his image, you are a person of purpose and destiny. You are not subject to the whims of other people or their wrong choices. As one who is taking on this victor mentality, God wants you to grow in your knowledge of him by immersing yourself in his Word. If you don't already, I encourage you to start reading the Bible every day for yourself.

## A Beginning Bible Reading Plan

- Start in the New Testament and read one chapter a day beginning in the book of Matthew. Continue to read through the whole New Testament.
- Also, from the Old Testament, read one chapter from the Book of Proverbs and one chapter from the Book of Psalms. I still do this daily because I receive wisdom and encouragement from these two books.
- If you desire to read more, read one chapter from the Book of Genesis and read through the whole Old Testament.
- I suggest you read from the New International Version or the New Living Translation to begin with.

You will grow and mature so much as you read the Bible and start learning and obeying what you read.

God wants you to know the riches of your inheritance in the saints. The Bible is the will—the legal document—that explains everything that belongs to you. And the only way you know what belongs to you is to get to the will and read it. I don't know anyone who's been left a will and didn't open it. Get to the will right away and find out what belongs to you and who you are in Christ Jesus. It can be the difference between life and death. The Word is who you are; let *this* mentality be in you.

Philippians 2:5 says, "Let this mind be in you which is in Christ Jesus." Then Romans 13:12 says, "Put on the Lord Jesus Christ and make no provision for the flesh." Make no provision—no room—for self-pity. Make no provision for a victim mentality. You have a choice.

The Bible says, "Put on the new man who is renewed in knowledge" (Col. 3:10, NKJV). You are a new person in Christ Jesus. Ephesians 4:22 says, "Put off the former self." Put off that victim mentality. It's time to put off the former self, the former thoughts, and put on the new. It's time to put off saying, "Why me?" It's time to stop blaming others. It's time to stop relying on people for contentment. It's time to stop living from a place of fear and having a negative self-image. It's time to stop complaining and feeling powerless and seeing yourself as weak. It's time to stop remaining in the same thought patterns and being critical, bitter, and stuck. It's time to put that old nature, that old person, off and put on the new person you are in Christ.

That new person is blessed, chosen, and adopted. They are a redeemed person, forgiven and marked with the Holy Spirit. They are a person who has been lavished with the grace of God. That new person is you!

So put off the old and put on the new. Start growing in the knowledge of God. Realize your inheritance and starting walking in it.

When God brought the Israelites out of Egypt, he did it with many signs and wonders. The first obstacle they came up against was the Red Sea. They were trapped. They looked in front of them and there was the Red Sea. They looked behind them, and there was Pharaoh and all his chariots and horsemen. The people panicked and thought they were doomed. They were indeed between a rock and a hard place.

To calm them down, Moses said to them, "Do not be afraid. Stand firm and you will see the deliverance the Lord will bring you today. The Egyptians you see today you will never see again. The Lord will fight for you; you need only to be still" (Exod. 14:13–14). But then God must have picked up something in Moses' spirit. Perhaps he gathered as much faith as he could to tell the people to stand still, but deep in his heart, he was still shaken and afraid. So God said to him, "Why are you crying out to me? Tell the Israelites to move on. Raise your staff and stretch out your hand over the sea to divide the water so that the Israelites can go through the sea on dry ground" (vv. 15–16).

God had to help Moses get his fight back. He forgot that he had the supernatural rod of God in his hand. God was saying to Moses, "You stretch out the rod. I'm not going to do it for you. I have given you all you need. I gave you a weapon. I gave you a rod. I turned it into a snake. I sent all of those plagues. Don't you know by now that I'm going to work on your behalf? Don't you know, Moses, that if I delivered you back then I will deliver you today and I will deliver you tomorrow? Why are you still crying to me?"

Can't you hear God calling out to you in a similar way? He's saying, "Why are you still crying to me? Don't you know I got this? Don't you know I'm going to deliver you? Just be still. Just be quiet. I will fight your battles for you."

Moses may have forgotten for a moment what he had in his hands, but you can allow his experience to remind you of mighty weapons you have in your hands. You have the name of Jesus, so use it. Boldly declare what God's Word says over your situation. God said that you can speak to your mountain and see it cast into the sea. Do it, even now. Rise up in the strength of God and fight the good fight of faith and God will partner with you to bring you victory over your enemies.

I love the end of this story of Moses and the people of Israel. Somehow, I had overlooked its ending in the past. The Bible says, "Then the angel of God, who had been traveling in front of Israel's army, withdrew and went behind them. The pillar of cloud also moved from in front and stood behind them, coming between the armies of Egypt and Israel. Throughout the night the cloud brought darkness to the one side and light to the other side; so neither went near the other all night long."

Isn't that amazing? The cloud brought light to the Israelites, but it brought darkness to the enemy. This is showing us that God will put a barrier between you and the enemy. When you have light, the enemy will have darkness. In other words, when you have peace, the enemy will have confusion. God is putting up barriers around you, and as you trust him, he is fighting for you. It's only right to answer back to him in faith and get your fight back. Get back in the game. You're not a victim. You're a victor. This is your time to shine.

Isaiah 60:1 says, "Arise [from spiritual depression to a new life], shine [be radiant with the glory and brilliance of the Lord]; for your light has come, and the glory and brilliance of the Lord has risen upon you" (AMP).

No more secrets. No more victim mentality. It's time to arise from your spiritual depression to the new life God has given you. The brilliance of the Lord is rising upon you even right now. Take hold of this now. Reclaim what is yours. It's in your inheritance as God's child to see all that God has promised you delivered. Rejoice and take courage. Keep your eyes off of your problems and look to Jesus. Trust him and believe that from the day you prayed, God released your answer. What you have been waiting for is on the way!

## PRACTICAL APPLICATION

*Encouraging thoughts and scriptures to meditate on:*

- I choose the life and blessings that God has made available to me. Deuteronomy 30:19 says, "I have set before you life and death, blessings and curses. Now choose life."

- Nothing can keep me from my purpose and from living an abundant life. Proverbs 21:30 says, "There is no wisdom, no insight, no plan that can succeed against the Lord."

- I am a victor because God causes me to triumph in Christ Jesus! Second Corinthians 2:14 says, "Now thanks be to God who always leads us in triumph in Christ, and through us diffuses the fragrance of His knowledge in every place."

*Practical steps I can take:*

- I will put off a victim mentality and live as the victor God wants me to be.

- I will put on the Lord Jesus Christ and be renewed in my mind and transformed in my thinking.

- I have my fight back and I will not give up because victory is on the way!

# Acknowledgments

Writing this book has been an amazing journey taken with the help of many friends and loved ones. I am extremely thankful for the wonderful people instrumental in making this project possible and enjoyable.

My heartfelt thanks to Daisy Hutton and Beth Adams, our friends at FaithWords, for helping make my dream come true.

I am grateful for our friends Jan Miller and Shannon Marven at Dupree/Miller for believing in this project. Thank you for your encouragement, wisdom, and hard work.

I am blessed to have worked with Jevon Bolden, a gifted wordsmith, who helped make this book what it is.

I am immensely blessed with the unending support and encouragement of my wonderful husband, Kevin, and our three children, Catherine, Caroline, and Christopher, who I love and treasure with all my heart.

Thank you to my daddy, the late Pastor John Osteen, who taught me to never give up because God is always faithful.

# About the Author

Lisa Osteen Comes is a bestselling author, podcast host, and associate pastor at America's largest church, Lakewood Church in Houston. Lisa's passion for God's Word and love for people radiate in her practical, yet insightful messages. Lisa is a graduate of Oral Roberts University. She is married to Kevin and they have three grown children. Connect with Lisa on Facebook, Twitter, Instagram, or visit her website at lisaosteencomes.com.